I LOVE SEX, I LOVE MYSELF

UNMASKING SEXUAL DEPRESSION, HEALING AND WINNING THE BATTLE WITHIN

LAVENDER JONES M.D.

Contents

Introduction   v

1. How to Understand a Sexually Active Person Post Sexual Trauma   1
2. Why People Hide from Society After Sexual Trauma   15
3. Sexual Damage from Sexual Trauma   33
4. Regaining Healthy Sexuality   52
5. Being Free and Breaking Away from Depression   69

Final Thoughts   93
Sources   99

Introduction

One out of every nine females and one out of every fifty-three males have suffered some type of sexual trauma, according to the Rape, Abuse, & Incent National Network (RAINN), 2016. The report cites that every 1 ½ minutes someone is assaulted sexually and every 8 minutes one of those victims is a child (RAINN, 2016). The terrible news here is that these are the statistics of only those reported. The significant degree of shaming, stigma, and blaming surrounding sexual assault and childhood sexual trauma prevents many victims from coming forward.

Many in the field of preventative sexual violence argue that the United States has a rape culture! What they mean by rape culture is not about a group of people or one person but an attitude adopted by a society that negates the impact, minimizes, or maintains sexual violence (Peterson, 2008). The good news is that awareness and change are on the horizon. I lived this horrible truth as a child, and over time I was able to conquer it but it was hard! I chose to write this book because the world is changing and it isn't anywhere close to where I was as a kid. So, I want to do everything in my power to make people and the societies within which we live more aware, open to acceptance, and confidence in themselves! In nearly all of the scholarly articles, case studies, statistical analyses, in the literature in the past five years, trauma, trauma-based interventions, and trauma-informed care were mentioned. However, I did not seem to come across a great deal of information shared about how couples heal when one of them is a survivor of sexual violence, so I intend to fully discuss that aspect, as well.

The purpose of this book is to provide closure and a sense of freedom from being trapped within yourself due to sexual abuse, assault, childhood trauma, etc. I want people to understand that they are not alone, and someone is always there to help them move forward as well as help others with similar situations. Another purpose for writing this book is to present a foundational level of training skills that you can apply what you learned to your own life experiences, and get satisfying results. This book will help you or anyone you know who has been sexually traumatized somewhere in your or their lifetime. A lot of people find it hard to cope with sexual trauma, as well as being themselves around others or alone. Understanding the severity of being trapped within yourself with no outlet is key to understanding and maintaining recovery. We all want to be respected as an individual in society without any backlash from our past.

In this book, you will learn how to enable and empower yourself to gain control back into your life from sex addiction, porn addiction, the trauma of molestation, being raped, or any other form of sexual violence you or a person with whom you care about has experienced. You will learn you're not alone in the world. Starting from a blank slate to understanding who you are today, and how to capitalize on being happy sexually, this book will help you regain control of your freedom from sexual discomfort without feeling down about who you are.

As a survivor of sexual trauma learns how to heal and recover, many will face the struggles with negotiating and discussing sexual intimacy. It is all about baby steps and learning to love yourself first. Many of us struggle with intimacy, codependency, or the other extreme and have numbed out those feelings and therefore, have been left with a sexual addiction or turning to the life of a sex worker. Wherever you may fall or someone you care about may fall on this continuum, a life of freedom, happiness, and wholeness is waiting for you, if you are willing to do the work.

My name is Lavender Jones, M.D. Over the years of study, experience, and conversations with many survivors, I have learned the answers to many of the questions sought by survivors of sexual assault, incest, rape, humiliation, and body shaming and the steps toward overcoming past trauma. It may be hard for most to grasp or believe in the concept of freedom when it comes to being sexually abused or assaulted, but the truth does set you free.

Whether you're male or female, being sexually attacked is traumatic for anyone. That's why I have devoted my life to helping others to overcome what I once encountered in my life! I want to show people that no matter how you are feeling, the steps to overcoming will be as effective as they are rewarding. Once you have taken control of your thoughts as well as gaining increased self-esteem you will start to feel more comfortable with yourself as an individual. Trust and respect are core characteristics of a person whether they're single or in a relationship. Training your mind to excel over insecurities and past trauma will earn you self-respect and the respect of others.

Ever heard the saying "old habits die hard?" Well... It's true, especially when it comes to training your emotions. Your mind is like a sponge that is willing and ready to take control of your life again if you are willing to do a bit of work. Understanding old habits and creating new ones can be a challenge, but it's just like learning to ride a bike, take steps today, and stop listening to negative self-dialog or other people that don't have your best interest at hand. These methods and strategy tips that you're about to read are proven to yield incredible results within yourself. NO MATTER

THE SITUATION. Each chapter in this book will provide you with actionable steps that will help you to get rid of depression as well as repression. Understanding and loving yourself are the best attributes of self-respect. If you follow the training in this book, it is very likely that you will have the tools necessary to never fall back into toxic shame, depression/repression, etc.... again.

A fulfilling and happy sex life is important to your health and wellness for many reasons. Emotional and physical elements of healthy sexuality have far-reaching benefits, including stress reduction, a healthier heart, and lower blood pressure. Sex is also a fun and natural part of life. However, for the survivor of sexual violence, sex can be a great source of worry and anxiety. Sex therapy is a multidisciplinary approach to eliminating and treating the struggles associated with trauma. It is important to have a complete physical examination to rule out any underlying medical concerns prior to getting treatment for sexual concerns. Sex therapy can help you and if you have a partner, a way to have honest and open communication so you can work through any issues related to your trauma and achieve a happy and healthy sex life.

ONE

How to Understand a Sexually Active Person Post Sexual Trauma

When someone uses threats, force, or emotional blackmail to conduct an unwanted sexual activity, they are known to be a sexual predator. Most of the time perpetrators of sexual crimes know their victims and often have earned their trust. Immediately a victim of such abuse will feel intense fear, shock, or disbelief, but in the long run, acute anxiety disorders, addiction, and post-traumatic stress disorder (PTSD) are among the many problems often affecting the survivors. All evidence considered in the treatment of sex offenders remains unpromising, at best, treatment protocols and crisis interventions for survivors are becoming increasingly effective.

Regardless of how old a person is or their gender, sexual violence impacts an individual far past any of the physical injuries. The emotional trauma of being sexually assaulted or raped can be life-shattering, leaving the person feeling alone, ashamed, and in fear. Flashbacks, nightmares, and traumatic memories create an environment that never feels safe for a survivor of rape, incest, or any other form of sexual trauma. It is seemingly impossible to trust another person and sometimes you don't even trust yourself.

I had trouble distinguishing what was in response to trauma and what was real. You may have low self-worth and even question your sanity and judgment. Self-blaming, feeling dirty or damaged, and thinking intimacy is a dangerous place to go, are common feelings for the survivors of sexual violence. The most important thing for you to realize is that what you are experiencing are normal reactions to sexual trauma.

The good news is that blaming yourself, feeling defective and helpless are NOT reality. As difficult as it must seem, there are strategies and techniques that will help you come to terms with the unfortunate circumstances in your life so you can regain your sense of trust and safety, and learn how to heal and move forward in your life.

The truth is that you were not dealt the best hand in life, but using that hand to find your purpose is all you need to live a happy, healthy, and productive lifestyle. Understanding that you're not alone and so many others have beat the odds that you seek answers for. I believe this method will open a lot of eyes and minds to those who are walking in the dark from sexually traumatized events. All things considered, hearing someone open up about their past can release a lot of negative toxins from within yourself as well as in others.

Understanding a Sexually Active Individual

Understanding what it means to be a healthy sexually active person takes a holistic perspective. Psychological, emotional, physical, intellectual, and spiritual dimensions are all part of the human experience. Integrating healthy sexuality into your life is an endeavor that takes balance and development over the course of a lifetime.

The following are considered to be characteristics of a healthy sexually active individual:

Communication

- Respectful and appropriate interaction with all genders
- Effective communication with friends and family
- When or if necessary, asking other adults appropriate questions regarding sexual issues.
- Ability to negotiate and communicate terms and limits for sexual encounters.
- Respectfully able to express your desire to engage in sex or not to engage in sex
- Doesn't feel insulted or hostile when someone refuses to have sex.
- Can express yourself physically, feelings of desire and attraction that are not focused on the genitals, such as hugging, kissing, caressing, etc.
- Have an open discussion with your partner(s) about what your relationship intentions are, such as friendship, dating, marriage, etc.
- Ability to respect others' limits and boundaries.
- Sensitivity to non-verbal gestures related to the limits and boundaries of others.

Relationships

- The ability to have friendships without an agenda that includes sex
- Does not exploit partner in any way
- Chooses responsible, safe, trustworthy, and giving partners
- Can engage in emotional intimacy without physicality, such as discussions about sexual desires, wants, and needs.
- Develop friendships that do not have a sexual agenda.
- Take responsibility for your own personal boundaries.

- Knows appreciation for your own body
- Can touch your own body without any disgust or shame
- Comfortable experiencing sexual and sensual pleasures
- Appreciate their own bodies
- Allows yourself to be nurtured by others and to practice self-love
- Know the difference between touch rather than sex
- Self-understanding
- Comfortable with sexual orientation and identity
- Growing awareness of the impact of sexual trauma and societal maladaptive patterns toward sexual violence.
- Allowing yourself to be vulnerable.
- Comfortable setting boundaries
- Start addressing issues related to past experiences

Understanding Sexual Repression/Depression

For many individuals, sexy thoughts inspire anticipation or excitement around possible sexual experiences in the future or warm and fuzzy past encounters. Spending time on these thoughts may leave you feeling aroused and possibly lead to masturbation, which is totally normal! However, if you are struggling with repressing sexual thoughts, just thinking of the word "sex" can trigger shame or embarrassment.

Some people learn from a very early age that sex is only for procreation, marriage, or that it is painful or unpleasant. Maybe you were taught that touching yourself is a sin and that if you masturbate you will go to hell. The worst-case scenario is that you experienced discomfort or trauma with parts of your body and your mind at such a young age that you didn't even know that should never happen. As a result of any of the aforementioned scenarios regarding your sexuality, you have learned to

4

repress your completely natural feelings and desires to protect yourself.

If you have found yourself suffering from sexual repression, you may also suffer from a host of emotional and physical issues including low self-worth, aggression, chronic fatigue syndrome, insomnia, and/or chronic irritability. Simply put, sexual repression is the inability to express your natural sexuality in a self-fulfilling manner.

Sexual repression causes your drives, urges, and sexual instincts to be stunted. It can affect you in a way that you are either completely uninterested in sex or overly interested in sex. I often wonder these days, how come people seem to be A-okay with watching slasher flicks but are so uncomfortable with watching any graphic sex scenes. Children's video games are riddled with guns and other killing machines! But, letting a child see a naked butt? No way!! The answer is in societal conditioning not only from parents, but our religious affiliations, media, and even the educational system.

Religious-based institutions have laid the foundation for what is considered acceptable or "right" and what is considered inappropriate or "wrong". Sexual repression or depression is about thinking sex is immoral, dirty, and awful to be a part of. And if you're like me, you've bought into these beliefs big time. Depending on how you were raised and what your religious environment was like you may have been taught that sex is dirty or that if two men or two women are together sexually, they are an abomination and that God will punish anyone who has sex outside of marriage.

I had a friend growing up that was told the old adage that if you masturbate you will grow fur on your hands. I knew a girl whose father told her that women who wear miniskirts deserve to get raped. Most people who experience erotic wounds started with early childhood dysfunction. Even in the 1960s, TV marriages slept in separate beds. The reality is that most people are poorly educated when it comes to sex, many were punished, shamed, rejected, and abused as children for such things as playing 'doctor' or touching their own genitalia.

Sadly, those shameful reactions from parents, teachers, religious leaders, and the like towards sexuality in a person's early years molds perceptions about sex in teenage and adult lives. You nor myself certainly weren't ashamed about getting our diapers changed, so it had to be learned somewhere. The following are some examples of sexual repressions based on early childhood experiences:

- Shame around any form of nudity
- Discomfort or shock when viewing anything sexual on TV or in the movies.
- Shaming you for sexually expressing yourself in any way (i.e., You dirty boy, take your hand off of there!")
- Dirty, bad, and/or wrong labels for sex (Dirty magazines).
- Anything having to do with sexuality is a family secret
- Stiff gender roles
- Punishment for any type of sexual expression.

Porn Addiction

There are varying opinions about whether or not porn addiction is a diagnosable mental illness or merely a public health concern. However, it is a rapidly growing industry on a global scale. Porn websites are visited by approximately fifty million Americans, regularly, and about 30 percent of downloads on the Internet are porn-related (Hairston, 2021). As with alcohol or drug addiction, individuals who progress to using porn due to increased stress levels or to escape reality, suffer many of the same negative consequences. Some porn addicts are so enthralled with viewing sexual acts online, in print, or on adult pornographic television sites that their life has become unmanageable. Also similar to drug addiction, a person's brain experiences a surge in levels of dopamine to the point of dependency, and therefore they lack the ability to control their behaviors about when, where, how, and why, they compulsively have to watch porn.

The brain has started to demand its porn fix stimulation. When a certain period of time passes without the stimulation, a craving arises, similar to that of a physical withdrawal. The brain has become so desensitized to ordinary sexual stimuli or sensual arousal that it requires a habitual dopamine boost. Some people wonder if they are porn-addicted just because they watch some X-rated movies over a period of time. The question here is, when does porn become an addiction? Just because someone enjoys viewing their favorite porn movies doesn't mean they need addiction treatment. Here are some common signs of pornography addiction:

- Ignoring responsibilities to watch porn
- Shame when viewing erotic films but still continue to watch them.
- Lying about watching porn
- Feeling humiliated or embarrassed due to obsessive porn watching.
- Needing to watch more and more extreme porn to get the same sense of erotica, such as moving from soft-porn to hard-core, or excessive exploitation of pornography starts.
- Spending excessive money on porn at the cost of your other needs. Moving from free samples to spending a chunk of change to get more. Remember, the porn industry is BIG business. They have marketing strategies that rival seeing a juicy Big Mac when you're hungry. The more you browse, the more tantalizing they become.
- Risk-taking to watch porn. Triggers can set you to tapping your cell for a quick fix at inconvenient places such as work or school. Beware of Popups triggering you to tap onto your favorite porn site. Maybe you think it will go

unnoticed, but the excitement will be written on your face and your work will be affected. Getting fired for watching porn at work is an embarrassing problem to have.

- Less satisfying sex life with your partner. People addicted to porn usually become habitual masturbators. When you get used to the grip of your hand or the sensation of a vibrator, a lover may not be able to give you the same intensity, leaving climax by intercourse difficult. Also, many fantasies that porn supplies are not realistic for a "normal" relationship. People have destroyed many good relationships chasing fantasies.
- Inability to stop watching porn. You want to stop but feel like you can't.
- Feeling a sense of anger or rage when asked to cut down or stop watching porn.

Being Damaged Sexually

Hypersexuality or sex addiction is a compulsive behavior that causes you discomfort, is difficult to control and affects your mental health, employment, relationships, or other important aspects of your life. Sometimes, these compulsions are in the form of cyber-sex, masturbation, payment for sex, multiple sexual partners, and porn. If any of these behaviors become disruptive to your life and are difficult to manage, you may be damaged sexually. If left untreated, the result can be low self-esteem, loss of employment, health problems, and relationship problems.

Both women and men can be damaged sexually by compulsive activities. Advances in technology have made access to sexual imagery much easier. It is easier to act out compulsive sexual behaviors in privacy or secrecy making them become worse over time. While some studies indicated that the severity or nature of the abuse may affect the degree of damage sexually in adulthood many other factors influence the extent of the damage inflicted by sexual violence. Such factors as a support network, internal coping strategies, and the survivor's perspective all play a part in what it means to be damaged sexually and what recovery looks like.

Not all forms of sexual damage are from direct touch, childhood sexual violence can come in many forms of exploitation. Showing a young child pornography, Internet assault, taking inappropriate photographs are all ways children's basic rights are infringed upon. Children have the right to develop sexually at the appropriate time that is within their choices and their control. When it is forced upon them, the child becomes traumatized and the normal psychosocial growth is impeded. People suffering from depression often are damaged sexually, as depression is the more frequently occurring long-term symptom of childhood sexual abuse.

Survivors have trouble externalizing the trauma, therefore believing shameful or negative feelings about themselves. With many years of negative thoughts about themselves, survivors can be left feeling devalued and avoidant of other people because they feel undeserving of anyone's time. The guilt, shame, and low self-worth can lead to a feeling that life just isn't worth living. Problems with food happen as well as body image disturbances for those who have been violated sexually as a child. If someone you trusted was your abuser, it may be difficult to view them as a perpetrator, so turning the blame inward tends to happen. Addiction and personality disorders, as well as self-destructive behaviors, are mentioned frequently in the literature regarding childhood sexual violence (King, 2009; Long et al., 2006; Maltz, 2002). Feeling ugly and dirty plague survivors who remain secretive about their abuse.

Narcissism

Narcissism is a relevant subject in the area of trauma associated with sexuality. Devaluing the self leaves the survivor in a state of depression and submission and sometimes the only role known is the victim. The definition of narcissism in the DSM-V focuses on the individual's tendencies for grandiosity, arrogance, rage, and exploitativeness, but if you pay attention to the less talked about characteristics of the narcissist, you will find features correlating with the personality of the abuser, such as shame sensitivity, vulnerability, anxiety, introvertedness. It is common for the abused to assume some characteristics of their abuser, narcissism being one of them.

Narcissistic characteristics stem from early childhood environments that were less than ideal, where abuse or neglect occurred, or too much attention or lack of boundaries were present. Similar to an abusive parent, an over-involved parent doesn't view their child as a unique and separate individual, but an unrealistic or idealized version of the child. Likewise, the abusive parent devalues the child and therefore, also has an unrealistic image of their child. Either way, the maltreatment leaves the individual constantly searching for other people to meet their needs, so they can get what they never had.

Playing the role of a victim can be a substitution for having a real or true identity. In a group therapy session, I heard a survivor say "I am the one that was sexually abused, most people haven't had that happen". But, the longer I listened to this person, I realized, (as did they later in treatment) that no one could ever do enough. When you harbor resentments, you block any type of supportive help. This way of reasoning turns into a person's perspective on life and usually creates maladaptive behavior patterns. Some traumatized people end up with narcissistic traits because they have built their identity around victimhood.

For some, it was the only choice when faced with an early experience of feeling non-existent. When grown, the victim can start relationships where mistreatment is the familiar way of doing things. When someone feels defective, they can compensate with grandiosity and organize their thought schema as being more powerful than others or better than.

Sexual Narcissism vs Narcissistic Sexual Behaviors

Sexual narcissism should not be confused with someone who has narcissistic sexual traits, they do sound almost exactly alike. Here is the difference:

1. Sexual narcissism is not a mental health disorder.
2. Sexual narcissism refers to characteristics that are only exhibited in sexual activities or their attitude about sex.
3. Narcissistic personality disorder has nothing to do with sexual narcissistic traits.

Sex with a Narcissist

In the beginning, narcissists seem considerate, passionately devoted, and very interested in pleasing you sexually. Maybe they lavished you with compliments, promises of love, gifts, and attention to the point you may have had a hint they were coming on strong. However, with time, you started to notice a red flag here and a red flag there. The following are some red flags to know if you are in bed with a narcissist

- They slowly start to criticize and devalue you.
- They begin to ignore you and then lash out in anger when you do or say something they don't approve of.
- They no longer seem to care what gives you sexual pleasure, but instead are only focused on their own desires.
- They tend to need constant praise and the act entitled.
- They start acting in bed the same way they act out of bed.
- Cuddling and touching go out the window.
- There are no intimate feelings after their narcissism is revealed, they weren't real, to begin with.
- They get bored when you want to talk about feelings and they will quickly change the subject to being about them.

- They consider themselves sexually gifted and most important.
- They want you to make sure you please them to orgasm, and really don't care if you have one. That said, self-importance can also mean that they could want to satisfy you so you can praise their skills and tell them how considerate they are as a partner.
- They may want to please you so you will brag or praise them. So, they may want you to describe in detail what they did to make you feel good and how much you enjoyed it.
- They need praise after every time you have sex. If you don't praise their performance, they will sulk or become passive-aggressive.
- Get angry if you disagree about wanting to have sex or you don't want them to do certain things, for instance, "I don't like it when you bite my neck" "Please don't hold the back of my head down when I am down there". Instead of appreciating your openness they will dismiss your expressions and start to point out personal flaws and make mean remarks. For instance, "I only hold your head in place because you don't know what you're doing".

Narcissists believe they are entitled to have you whenever they please and think that you are always waiting for them. When you are not in the mood for sex, they may try to lay a guilt trip on you, accuse you of cheating, resort to name-calling, compare you sexually to someone from their past, or tell you they are going to "do it" with someone else. You may not see this as abuse and may start to question yourself. For the trauma sufferer, it can be like a ghost from the past because this type of manipulation falls under the pretense of sexual coercion. They are calculated steps to make you give in to their wants and feel bad about yourself at the same time. No person deserves or is entitled to having sex with you. It is normal to feel a bit disappointed when your lover is not in the mood, but if your relationship is healthy, you should be able to identify with that feeling and not take it personally. Likewise, if you are not in the mood, your partner will respect your boundaries and your decision, and in no way pressure you into changing your mind.

Narcissists usually lack the ability to feel empathy. That doesn't make them totally incapable of understanding someone else's feelings, but it does mean they really don't think about how their behaviors affect you. They may not even seem aware of your feelings. If you are living with a narcissist, you may start to feel that as long as you give them what they want, that is all that matters. Commonly, they have a very specific and detailed outline of exactly how your relationship should play out. They will let you know exactly what they expect of you. This includes in the bed; what to wear, what position to assume, and even what to say. They have no interest in your opinion. You may start feeling objectified and less of a partner.

Narcissistic behaviors usually exist on a spectrum. Someone may have some of the traits or varying degrees of the traits. Some narcissistic characteristics are less severe and may respond with more willingness to consider your feelings if you call them out. Those who only have narcissistic characteristics may not have a diagnosable narcissistic personality disorder and can actually come around and learn to consider their emotions and sexual desires. There are also narcissistic subtypes. That means the person has some of the main traits, but they vary from person to person.

A lot of people can have an exaggerated sense of self-importance and superiority. Many people can be grandiose, at times. However, if someone exhibits grandiose narcissism they might:

- Demand sex outright
- Disagree with any of your challenges of their behaviors
- Come right out and tell you to praise them

- Show rageful behavior at the first mention of any criticism and can become openly enraged when you disagree

People who carry narcissistic traits do have a tendency to be unfaithful, it's not an automatic cheat, and they may never be sexually coercive or aggressive, but they will usually only care about their own feelings with little regard for anyone else's.

TWO

Why People Hide from Society After Sexual Trauma

Society as a whole is far from understanding how victims react to sexual violence. Unfortunately, these misconceptions also persist in the educational, judicial, and political systems. More importantly, we as a society have to press the question as to why victims of sexual assault hide from society or remain silent about their abuse. Shame is the most common reason for survivors to hide from society. Being sexualized as a child is dehumanizing and humiliating.

Feeling helpless and being invaded at the hands of another person is degrading and makes a person, especially a child, feel helpless and hopeless. Loss of control anxiety sets in and is quickly manifested as toxic shame. Once toxic shame is in the picture, the victim is essentially blaming themselves for the perpetrator's behavior. Feeling responsible for these treacherous actions is what causes individuals to hide or not speak up. People hide when feeling ashamed. Isolation puts the victim far away from society, which translates into further low rates of sex violence reporting.

Another cause for not reporting or hiding from society is that trauma can mess up your memory. When it first happens, you may be too young to remember the sequence of violent experiences, or if you learned to dissociate, it can be difficult to keep the memories from becoming fragmented. This is the brain's way of trying to cope with sexual traumatization. The person isn't doing it on purpose. Sometimes, when trying to recall or discuss a traumatic experience, it may seem like the story doesn't add up. This is NOT the victim's fault.

The cognitive part of the brain shuts down during the attack as its only means of coping with what is unbearable (Karlos, 2019). So, a process of fragmentation occurs. If people don't know this about sexual abuse, they tend to disbelieve the victim. And the cycle of misunderstanding repeats itself. It's not that the victim doesn't remember the pain of the attack, but the order of the events when they happened can be scrambled. The absolute fear of not being believed makes the victim hide from society or not report the abuse.

One of the most unfortunate reasons people hide after sexual abuse is due to society's stigmatization! In a rape culture, sexual abuse is normalized, and the associated violence is minimized and the blame falls upon the victim "So and so asked for it". Victims are marginalized making it easier to hide than to face the blame game. This reasoning also lets the abuser off the hook, so to speak, as they are not held accountable for their actions. This makes the victim hide even more because they don't feel their abuser will face any consequences. It's hard to imagine that a person can suffer such an atrocity and be blamed for it. According to the Rape, Abuse and Incest National Network (2016), "out of every 1000 rapes, 994 perpetrators will walk free."

Victims also hide from society because they believe the police force doesn't take their stories seriously. As victims, we learned to live in fear. Fearing the perpetrators may retaliate if reported against Some parents who have sexually abused their children threaten financial abandonment or throwing them out of the house before they are old enough to fend for themselves. The perpetrator is already viewed as all-powerful even though it is not true. This is the way it is for sexual abuse, especially in the workplace.

Blaming the victim sometimes comes with the sentiment that the person "doesn't act like a victim", as if there is an instruction manual on how to react to sexual assault. Each person reacts to sexual trauma differently. Society places expectations on victims such as being depressed or panic-stricken. Chances are if you look to your left and look to your right, you will find you never know who has been abused. Some may turn to self-medicating, some may withdraw completely from society, and some may work the streets and engage in sexual behaviors that are high-risk. All of these dysfunctional behaviors are the trauma victims' efforts to regain some sense of control in their lives. Sexual assault removes every bit of self-control a person has, so fear takes over and the victim will try to assume different personalities to try to hide their loss of control anxiety. For this reason, people think they do not act like a victim. Sometimes just the thought of being social after rape or molestation is traumatizing in itself. The reporting process is so awful, even if you know you are doing the right thing. So, if you ever wonder why someone doesn't tell you, maybe you have a better idea now.

Society goes to extreme lengths in blaming the victim, even as far as it happening because of the clothes they wear. This is another example of the rape culture and the distorted reality that comes with it. What does it say about the perpetrator who becomes violent over a pair of short shorts? How come this is not the million-dollar question? The whole idea of reporting abuse to a group of people in police uniforms, who are asking seriously personal questions, in a cold and emotionally removed environment, goes a long way in explaining why people don't come forward about being raped or molested, or sexually harassed. If the victim feels like the whole world doesn't believe them, they really don't see any point in telling. Society blames the victim, television, alcohol and drugs, everything and everyone except for the abuser! We must do better as a society. No survivor should ever be afraid to tell.

Sexual Abuse and Selling Your Body

Studies on the subject of sexual trauma in childhood consistently link the abuse to the victims starting prostitution (Durshlag & Goswami, 2008; Farley, 2003). According to the research, most individuals who engage in prostitution started sex work as adolescents. Victims already live in a state of fear, so the perpetual state of anxiety proposed in the area of sex work is a reality. It is a dangerous business with the possibility of facing violence again at the hands of a perpetrator. Living in a constant state of fear profoundly affects an already traumatized individual's daily life, decision-making processes, self-image, and ability to maintain control.

Internalizing circumstances that have happened to a sexually traumatized person is how they make sense of their life. So, in a distorted reality, consistent physical, sexual, and emotional threats are somewhat of the norm. The victim has come to believe that no person will ever take care of them and the only way they are worth anything is by giving sex. It is a lack of self-belief or empowerment. Individuals who prostitute themselves have multiple coping strategies for survival in a long-term oppressive and potentially violent atmosphere that epitomizes prostitution.

Another method employed for coping with childhood sexual abuse is escapism. Escapism is what happens when a victim turns to drugs and alcohol to numb the pain, fear, and emotional trauma from sexual assaults. Therefore, many people who have turned to prostitution also have their lives complicated with addiction. Temporarily, it is a means of escaping the immediate pain of selling one's body, and the chronic pain of traumatic memories.

One of the most pressing matters about prostitution is the ongoing violence is viewed upon as normal. Trafficking and prostitution are instances where human beings are hunted down, dominated, and sexually assaulted and harassed. Systematic brainwashing, physical control, and indoctrination are used against men and women prostitutes.

When reviewing the literature about the subject matter in this book, I found more articles talking about sexually transmitted diseases than I did on the violence and suicidality associated with prostitution (Farley, 2004; Herman, 2003). Homelessness, addiction, and a predominant factor of childhood sexual abuse precedes entry into sex work. Prostitutes are commonly victimized by customers, pimps, and intimate partner violence, through methods such as control and coercion. Like the batterers they knew as children, society is in denial of the sexual assault, physical violence, social deprivation, intimidation and threats, verbal assaults, and captivity that happen to sex workers on a daily basis (Stark & Hodgson, 2003).

By systematic acceptance of the violence perpetuated by the prostitution industry, individuals who already have low self-worth, stemming from childhood abuse, feel even more worthless, except when getting paid by a customer. Verbal abuse, early childhood trauma, teenage sexual assault, rape, battery, and torture, all of which are designations on the continuum of violence, and of which happen to prostitutes. Let's be clear, prostitution is trafficking. Trafficking is just the word for global prostitution.

Sex Abuse and Personal Insecurities

One of the most tragic results of being abused sexually is the negative way you think about yourself and the lack of understanding of what a healthy relationship looks like. After being forced to hide the truth throughout a lifetime, the victim's physical, emotional, and mental growth had to adapt to accommodate repeated isolation and terror from the unwanted invasion of their bodies. Sometimes, arousal is impossible to avoid. When this happens, the victim is left with an overwhelming sense of shame as their young minds are not developed enough yet to understand that something like friction can cause an erection and some things may feel pleasurable to the body that is very uncomfortable to the mind.

Similarly, trauma survivors must suffer the casualty of the meaning of consent. How, as an adult, do you have a healthy sex life if the very act triggers confusion and terror due to past horrors? Yet, I am here to tell you that I have witnessed the most inspiring and amazing desires in trauma survivors to heal; including myself! Victims of sexual violence have every right in the world to heal past the abuse and trauma and enjoy healthy sexual and intimate relationships.

Sexual trauma triggers strong negative feelings associated with any desire or action involving sex for survivors. When something is so frightening, the brain's flight/fight/freeze response occurs, and it happens unconsciously. We can't just turn it off, we have to learn how to feel differently about ourselves. I know people who turned to food and put on a tremendous amount of weight so they could create an actual physical boundary around themselves.

As survivors, we are hardwired to automatically "freak out" at the thought of engaging and hoping to enjoy a healthy adult sexual relationship. For the longest time, I had no hopes of enjoying intimacy. I only associated it with terror. But, with a bit of work on your inner child and some other therapeutic techniques, better days are ahead. No matter what difficulties or obstacles you may go through, you are not at fault. Even though you still may endure shameful and painful feelings, no matter what roadblocks or difficulties you may experience, they are not your fault. No matter what shame or pain you still endure, you can heal and move forward to find healthy love and wonderful sex.

You may ask yourself at times, what a healthy relationship looks like. It is one based on compassion, love, and caring and it is a place where you can go to find positive ways to experience your sexual desires, pleasure, and consent. They are a wonderful way for survivors to heal, and they are possible. Secure and safe attachments allow healing and enable you to have enjoyable sex. Committed relationships can be an important part of recovery because there has to be enough trust in your partner for you to reveal your past and feel safe doing it. Being able to ask for what you need, emotionally, and feeling safe while doing it, will help you to realize that your partner is really there for you. You can describe exactly what it means for you to feel safe and spell out your triggers in words that have meaning to your partner. Once you heal enough to learn and understand that sex and abuse are not the same thing, you can then begin to explore feeling a bit vulnerable and learn how to experience feeling sexually safe. First, you have to understand your needs so you can share them. Some of those needs may include:

- Leaving the lights on
- Picking the place where you want to have sex
- Having a set time
- Planning the lead-up such as massage or music, something relaxing, or an enjoyable routine for pre-sex.
- Making sure your partner understands that you want to be the initiator, to please understand that you have to go at your own pace and take the lead.
- Letting your partner know that you do not like for them to come up behind you or touch your neck in any way (know your triggers).
- Work together with a trauma specialist that helps you with the healing process and includes your partner. One that will teach you grounding and communication techniques.

What is Consent?

Sexual consent is a mutual agreement to engage in any type of sexual activity. In other words, you have to know if someone feels the same way you do. Be honest about exactly what you do and don't want to do. It is about setting personal boundaries and respecting the personal boundaries of others, and it also means making sure things are clear, and that doesn't just mean the first time, it means every time. Also, it doesn't matter what type of a relationship you are in. Your body is yours, so even if you were happy "doing it" in the past, or you are in a serious relationship, you can say "no" at any time.

Just because you are married or in a relationship doesn't imply ownership over your body. Likewise, if you are in a serious relationship and your partner isn't in the mood, show some respect and don't pressure anyone, ever, to do anything they don't feel like doing. Oral sex, touching someone's genitalia, and any type of vaginal, penial, or anal penetration is rape if there is no consent. Consent can be denied by just pushing someone away. You can deny consent without saying a word, you can pull away, look away, by simply disengaging from the person and what they are trying to do, you are denying consent. It is the Law!

Consent can't be implied by where you go or what you wear. There is no mystery or question, it is a clearly communicated consent. People under the age of 18 are protected by law from being talked into, manipulated, or pressured to have sex with someone who is much older. Adults who have sex with a minor (under the age of consent) face going to jail and being a registered sex offender for the rest of their lives. The laws vary in states about age, but if someone has to wonder what the laws ever are, there is a problem. Sometimes people are too frightened to say the word "no", and sometimes they enter a freeze response, which does not mean "yes".

If a person is intoxicated, and I don't mean sex after a couple of drinks, I mean inebriated, even if they seem to want to fool around, and they cannot communicate it clearly, err on the side of caution. If they can hardly stand up, or there is a chance they may not remember, it is a "NO". The best you can do is to make sure they stay safe. There isn't one single way for someone to commit sexual assault. They don't have to have a gun or a knife, the victim doesn't have to scream, fight back, or repeatedly yell "no", for it to be rape. In fact, most of the time the perp may be a romantic partner or someone the victim knows. If this has happened to you, you're not alone. Help is out there!

F.R.I.E.S.

- *Freely given*: Consent means choosing without any manipulation, pressure, or being intoxicated.
- *Reversible*: You can change your mind at any time about what you want and don't want to do. Even if you have already been with the person in the past, you can REVERSE your decision. Even if you are naked in bed with someone you can say NO or REVERSE your decision.
- *Informed*: You can only consent if you know the whole story. If someone tells you they are going to put on a condom and then they don't, you did not give consent.
- *Enthusiastic*: Sexually, only do the things you WANT to do. Never do something because you think it is expected.
- *Specific*: Saying yes to kissing is not saying yes to sucking or intercourse. Be specific.

Consent also means moving past preconceived notions regarding gender. There are no rules stating it is okay to pressure a man any more than it is to pressure or try to manipulate a woman. If you are in an intimate situation and things are heating up, here are some good ways to make sure there is consent before moving any further:

- Are you comfortable with how things are?
- Is this okay with you?
- Would you rather slow down?
- Do you want to stop?

Consent also means breaking away from preconceived notions of gender roles. There are no rules about who can initiate intimacy or who might want to take it fast or slow. The more comfortable you feel expressing your boundaries and desires, the more pleasurable your interactions together will be.

CONSENT EXAMPLES	Looks Like	Doesn't Look Like
You really want to give a kiss to that special someone, so you say "May I give you a kiss?"	The person looks at you, smiles, says "yes" and leans in for a kiss.	The person doesn't answer and looks away. They don't look comfortable.
You place your hand on that special someone's thigh	The person moves closer to you and smiles	The person moves away from you and brushes your hand off
You are in the middle of making out and you ask "Should we keep going?"	With enthusiasm, the person says "Yes!"	The person says "Maybe" but doesn't seem thrilled about it
You are in a heavy makeout session, but the person has had a lot to drink.	Wait until another day when the person is sober and they tell you, "Where were we?"	An intoxicated person cannot give consent
You want to have some casual sex with a friend	You have an open discussion about the possibility and both agree it is a great idea.	You know the person is looking to have a relationship with you and they tell you they have deep feelings.

Casual Sex: A Discussion

This is very much a discussion about casual sex. It depends on the people involved. There are a plethora of definitions in various scholarly journals, health and wellness websites, magazines, etc. I am going to present some of the pros and cons regarding the subject and leave it up to you to decide your own perspective about casual sex. There is no right or wrong point of view. Anyone who stands in judgment of others puts themselves in jeopardy o being judged. In a general sense, casual sex is consensual sex that is not part of a romantic relationship. To most, it means, no strings attached, or expectation of exclusivity or commitment (Wentland & Reissing, 2014). Common names for casual sex include friends with benefits, one-nighters, booty calls, trysts, hook-ups, and a variety of other euphemisms.

Contextually, casual sex can be everything from celebrated to stigmatized. Some consider casual sex very seriously both physically and emotionally, while others consider it to be, well, casual. That being said, there are strong opinions associated with the topic. Ironically, it seems to me that people's opinions tend to change according to their life circumstances. Whether or not you are more inclined to think lightly about the subject or you want to consider it down to every detail, it is helpful to understand a bit about the cultural perspectives and possible effect it has on your mental health when figuring out if it is right for you.

Casual sex can be a regular event or it might only happen once between partners. It may happen between two good friends, maybe with an ex, someone you date, here and there, or even a neighbor. It can happen spontaneously or it can be a scheduled activity. It is, in essence, a way to have the physicality of intimacy, without the emotional, romantic, or practical aspects of commitment or a love relationship. Some people find casual sex to be considered a normal part of their lives. Some individuals enjoy the lack of expectations, pressures, or accountability that comes with casual relationships, and that it is like a healthy form of exercise. For others, it is much more complicated as feelings can get hurt, and it is not so easy to manage the emotions involved without becoming attached (unrequited love). Either way, casual sex does carry the responsibility factor that comes with practicing safe sex. Unplanned pregnancies and sexually transmitted diseases (STDs), and the potential of emotional harm are some of the risk factors associated with casual sexual encounters.

Historically, casual sex has carried a sexist tone, especially when it comes to females. Cautionary tales of females losing their virtue are still part of many people's belief systems. Movies and television often portray casual sex as romps around the bedroom that sometimes ends in a love affair, and at other times ending in heartbreak and regret. Assumptions, stereotypes, morals, and personal ethics are all part of this ever-changing dynamic.

In addition, if someone has a bad casual sex experience, it may drastically sway their perspective on the subject. However, if you have a history of trauma, please consider the mental health consequences when making the decision as to whether casual sex is emotionally safe for you. There may be some benefits such as sexual satisfaction, but the emotional stress involved in casual sex may give you pause.

Society attaches a great deal of stigma to casual sex that can underly feelings of shame you may already be experiencing due to trauma. Consider how you may feel during and after the encounter before engaging in casual sex. It is difficult to have a trusting relationship with casual encounters. Many trauma victims take part in casual sex as a way to escape, bury, or avoid their feelings. Sexual trauma experiences have an impact on your central nervous system, so that even if you decide to have casual sex, your brain may trigger a sense of fight/flight/freeze, which is a neurochemical response. Whatever your decision is regarding casual sex, it is important to have consent and constant communication throughout any sexual activities.

Sex Addiction

Sex addiction by definition is the need to compulsively have sex in order to relieve an obsessional-type craving, much in the same way an addict needs "a fix" (Krueger, 2016). Sex addiction is a personal problem and should not be confused with other disorders such as bestiality or pedophilia. For some individuals, sex addiction can be very dangerous and result in considerable negative consequences. Like drug addiction or alcoholism, it can affect your mental and physical well-being. It has been reported to be widespread and some credible sources argue that it can go without being diagnosed, quite often (Healthline.com, 2021; Brody, 2010).

People with sex addiction are thought to have sex with multiple partners, even though this doesn't necessarily mean a person has a disorder. Commonly, when I hear people talking about sex addiction, it is usually in the form of habitual masturbation using porn. Again, sex addiction should not be confused with fetishes. Having an addiction of any type means seriously altering your life so you can compulsively do something multiple times a day; in this case, a sex act, even if there are serious negative consequences.

Sex addiction causes the person the inability to stop engaging in the behavior unless there is an intervention. It is usually characterized by a repetitive cycle of hypersexuality coupled with low self-esteem. While the act may bring relief, it is only short-term, while the negative psychological consequences get worse and increase over time. While sometimes, sex addicts get involved in bizarre sexual activities, it doesn't have to be. It simply means they cannot stop the behavior even when faced with detriment to themselves.

Someone suffering from a sex addiction faces various challenges that are unique to each individual. It can lead to actions that jeopardize your health, safety, and your relationships. Support groups and 12-Step Programs such as Sex Addicts Anonymous (SAA) follow the same approach to recovery as Narcotics Anonymous (NA) and Alcoholics Anonymous (AA). It is suggested to group members to refrain from destructive sexual activity, not to entirely give up sex. It is a very supportive atmosphere and can be very helpful in recovering from sex addiction. Cognitive *Behavioral Therapy* helps individuals to recognize sexual impulse triggers and teaches them how to alter unhealthy behaviors. CBT is an individual-type therapeutic regime. There are also inpatient sex addiction treatment programs. In this venue, individuals are to spend at least 30 days removed from their normal lives to aid them in regaining impulse control and start the recovery process.

People with sex addiction potentially engage in behaviors that can include, but are not limited to:

- Public Sex
- Sex Clubs
- Prostitution
- Consuming or watching porn
- Sexual fantasy while masturbating several times per day
- Voyeurism or exhibition
- Spending excessive time thinking about sex
- Obsessive fantasizing that interferes with personal responsibilities
- Spending excessive time looking for partners to fulfill a fantasy
- Excessive time spent having sex
- Feeling depressed, regretful, or shameful regarding sex
- Engaging in risky sexual activities
- Compulsive masturbation
- Masturbation during inappropriate times such as while driving or at work
- Masturbation to the point of causing physical discomfort or pain
- Cheating on partners
- Criminal Sexual activity

Anonymous Sex with a History of Trauma

There is no doubt that victims of sexual trauma have learned to numb out intrusive feelings, thoughts, and sensations. Additionally if the victim was violated by someone they trusted, distancing themselves during sex only seems natural. What better distance can you have during sex, than if you don't know the person; even their name. Being abused sexually, over a lengthy period of time causes developmental issues, one being a Sexual Desire Disorder (SDD) (Letourneau & O'Donohue, 1993). SDD results from an intense fear of bonding with another human being. It also leads to narcissism because the fear of bonding leads to an inability to empathize with others.

Frequently, people with SDD have learned to dissociate during sexual encounters, but another way to be disconnected is to have anonymous sex. Studies indicate that people who frequently have sex with strangers also suffer from sadness fear, and loneliness, as one would expect. Anonymous sex is not necessarily the same as casual sex. Some view casual sex as a healthy carnal outlet. Both casual and anonymous sex are considered risky. Trauma victims who practice anonymous sex often do so they remain unattached to the human aspect of the interaction. It only stands to reason that a rape victim or survivor of sexual trauma would experience difficulty regarding intimacy. Anonymous sex disrupts the mind's equilibrium in that by removing the emotion the person feels safer.

Even for those without a history of sexual trauma, up until recent times, people found anonymous sexual encounters in strip clubs, bars, and brothels. Most of the research I read about anonymous sex only referred to males in the past, such as gay men engaging in anonymous sex in public places like parks and bathrooms. The more recent literature points to finding anonymous sex via social media and apps on your smartphone. The Internet and sex-locater apps have permanently and drastically changed the landscape of anonymous sex.

With the influx of ways and the user-friendliness of technology, people with spotty track records don't have to run around in the darkness of night looking for prey any longer. Sexual compulsivity, cheating partners, and STDs must be on the rise as individuals mindlessly, while briefly, put their intimacy and health risks in the hands of a total stranger. There are those, though who enjoy the idea of sex without commitment and find a sense of freedom in anonymous sex. Who are we to judge? I can only write a cautionary tale, a warning to be careful out there.

What is Dissociating?

Dissociating is the mediating link between sexuality and trauma. It is a defense mechanism necessary for surviving the physical, emotional, mental, and spiritual violence associated with rape. I learned at an early age how to leave the reality of what was happening to me by taking myself somewhere else, anywhere else, even though it was only in my mind. By dissociating, I could turn myself into a robot and depersonalize the actions against me. If the victim becomes an object, it is easier to do what you're told.

Dissociation functions as a distancing tool because any feelings of closeness are too dangerous for the mind to bear. By taking the human element out of the act and essentially "going somewhere else", the victim is disengaged from their body, thereby, not able to feel or think about the trauma. It becomes such a part of you, that as time goes by, it seems to happen on its own. I often wondered why I had memory gaps or seemed to forget things. It didn't make any sense, as I was able to remember my studies enough to grad-uate medical school. As a survivor, I now know that it was a way to cope; if I wasn't real, then the world around me wasn't real. The following are symptoms of dissociation:

- Feeling like you are having an out-of-body experience
- Feeling like you are someone else
- Feel in a dreamlike state or light-headedness

- Feeling numb or not feeling any pain
- Having an altered sense of time
- Not knowing how you ended up somewhere else
- Experiencing tunnel vision
- Hearing voices that sound far away
- Experiencing harsh flashbacks that seem real, or as if they are happening in the current time.
- Become totally absorbed in a fantasy that feels real

Dissociative Warning Signs

- Difficulty remembering personal details
- Forgetting things, you have done or said
- Rapid mood swings
- Taking on other identities
- Panic attacks
- Depression
- Severe anxiety
- Suicidal ideation
- Addiction
- Treatment failures
- Children may seem to stare off in the distance, develop imaginary heroes, gaze out of the window for extended periods. **Some of these behaviors are normal for children, however, when coupled with a dysfunctional family environment, abuse may be occurring.

Dissociation as a Diagnosis

Once you have come to terms with needing help, your mental health physician will ask you about past experiences. If you have found yourself abusing substances, it is important to come clean with your doctor. A complete physical exam is required to rule out any medical illness or conditions as the cause for your dissociation. Brain scans to rule out any organic conditions may also be ordered. Most importantly, a referral to a mental health or trauma specialist should be issued. Treatment for Dissociative Disorders will be discussed further in the chapters related to Recovery for Sexual Trauma.

THREE

Sexual Damage from Sexual Trauma

The horrible truth is that some adults have too often made comments such as "He was too young when it happened to remember it when he grows up." Childhood sexual trauma has life-long effects. While children are resilient, they are not made of concrete. There are many different types of trauma experiences, and when it comes to those in childhood, it is characterized by events that threaten the child's body or their life. Sexual abuse is obviously traumatic, but so are other events such as car accidents, hurricanes, bullying, or medical crises. Also, characterized as sexual trauma is when the child witnesses sexual violence against another person.

One of the most damaging effects of childhood sexual abuse is the individual's inability to form and maintain deep, close, and trusting adult relationships on both an intimate and a platonic level (Kris-ense & Lau, 2014). Communication skills are impaired leading to difficulty expressing feelings to family and friends, and fear of talking about their past.

Being in a relationship can remind survivors of their past suffering and create emotional barriers making it difficult to discuss their abuse with someone with whom they want to be involved. I can remember before recovery feeling dirty talking about the past. Also, for me and some of my fellow survivors, there was tremendous fear that the sexual violence we suffered as children would affect being a parent (Foster & Hagedorn, 2014). Some victims have discussed not even being comfortable changing a baby's diaper.

Others have talked about becoming overly protective parents with their children and grandchildren. They want to make sure that their children never have to suffer or feel the pain they experienced as a child and can overcompensate to make sure their abuse doesn't affect their children's lives negatively. Another disturbing aspect of childhood sexual abuse is that the survivors may have trouble believing in spirituality or religion, especially if their abuser was affiliated with their religion or hypocritically practiced religion during the abuse. It is common for victims to feel disillusioned with spiritual practices after being assaulted sexually. Some may feel punished or abandoned by God or they may question the fact that a God could allow such a thing to happen to them. Oftentimes, a child can view their abuser as all-powerful like a God.

Some children are more affected than others by events that are traumatic, however, some develop post-traumatic stress disorder (PTSD). When a child develops PTSD, the trauma is re-experienced repeatedly in their minds, leading them to steer clear of any reminders of their trauma. Trauma experts use play therapy to help the child communicate their feelings and to tell what happened to them. Anxiety disorders can develop in children who have been abused and they become fearful of any warning signs that even hint that something awful may happen again.

The following are some of the problems that children with PTSD can potentially develop:

- Aggression and anger
- Depression
- Anxiety

- Trust issues
- Panic disorder
- Feelings of isolation
- Low self-esteem
- Self-destructive behavior

Even if a diagnosable PTSD is not evident, some of the behavioral and emotional issues to be on the lookout for include:

- Hostility
- Attention and focus problems
- Poor appetite
- Death anxiety
- Phobias
- Irritability
- Fear surrounding safety
- School phobias
- Physical complaints such as upset stomach and headaches
- Loss of interest in play or other activities development of a traumatized child can have long-term adverse effects on their health and wellness, including:
- Heart disease
- Asthma
- Diabetes
- High blood pressure
- Mental health problems
- Suicidal ideation

Getting help for a child you suspect has been abused is key to reducing the impact of sexual trauma. After notifying the proper authorities, here are some ways to help a child after an event that has resulted in anxiety, fear, trauma, and alongside professional assistance:

- Encourage the child to verbalize their emotions and validate their feelings.
- Answer any questions with clear and concise honesty
- Establish a trust that you will do everything in your power to keep them safe.
- Stick to normal routines

Some survivors shared with me that school was a good coping strategy, and then others shared that they could not pay attention in class due to the trauma. I can understand a young person feeling as if their abuser had stolen their future. College towns may seem like a threatening place to go, especially if it is a large school. Anxiety in crowds due to being overwhelmed and not knowing anyone can cause further difficulties for students who have been sexually traumatized. In fact, I believe every school should have educational programming on the topic, as you never know if there is a student coming to class who is severely struggling to try to get an education while suffering unresolved trauma issues. I strongly recommend educating students on sexual assault, especially childhood trauma and date rape. People need to be aware of what could happen, and what to do in those situations. I wish I had had an education and if I had, maybe I would have gone for help sooner. Kids need to know it isn't their fault.

Verbal Sexual Abuse

People can be sexually abusive in more ways other than physically. People are sexually abused through words and implications all of the time, including at work, online, and in the home. Sometimes people think they are being funny by making crude comments, but it is far from funny to talk about a person's body. People often act afraid to call someone out for talking "dirty" to them, they might be afraid of losing their job, being rejected, or losing an online buddy. Sex jokes, calling people nasty names, sexting without consent, teasing someone about their physical aspects, talking about sex graphically or in vivid detail, leaving inappropriate voice-mails, are just a few of the ways people are commonly verbally abused in a sexual manner. Whether you are in a romantic relationship or talking with your kids or parents, name-calling with sexual terms, such as "pussy" "asshole" and others, too awful to mention, are true methods of belittlement.

Some people use name-calling in their sex play. In this case, there needs to be an in-depth understanding between the two lovers about what is and isn't acceptable. I have heard in meetings where people have acquiesced to being called a "whore" or "cock-sucker" as a means of turning their partner on, just to realize later that it took a tremendous toll on them emotionally later. Then there are those people who have very powerful jobs they work in all day long, so they enjoy role-playing a more submissive role in the bedroom. Again, the main issue here is consent. Both people have to be turned on by the talk. If it is only pleasurable to one person, and not the other, then it is unhealthy. There has to be a truthful foundation for all sex.

The effects of sexual verbal abuse, especially on those under the age of 18, have long-term negative consequences. Children and teens can become very confused by sexual innuendos, and have trouble developing a sense of self-worth, and difficulty with making decisions. Ultimately, a person feels there is something wrong with them on a very basic level when they have grown up listening to people being objectified sexually, and tend to relive the abusive experiences, believing what was said. A study on the long-term effects of verbal abuse stated an association with chronic headaches, stuttering, irritable bowel syndrome, ulcers, and migraines, as well as heart problems (Holly, 2012). Verbal abuse, sexual abuse, and physical abuse usually go hand-in-hand. The more verbal abuse a child suffers, the worse the problems are later in life. Kids have a tendency to believe what their parents tell them.

The psychological effects of verbal abuse include:

- Depression
- PTSD
- Anxiety
- Toxic Shame
- Addiction
- Violence
- Eating disorders
- Exaggerated startle response
- Traumatic memories
- Suicide
- Memory problems
- Insomnia

Sexual Assault of Boys and Men

Sexual abuse can happen from perpetrators of any age, gender, race, socioeconomic status, gender identity, or sexual orientation, and they can be of any relationship to the victim. Like all perpetrators, they might use emotional or psychological coercion techniques or physical force. Of course, sexual trauma happens to people of all ages, genders, sexual orientations, and gender identity. Boys and men who have been traumatized sexually have in common many of the same reactions and emotions as other victims, however, they may face some additional struggles due to societal stereotyping and attitudes about masculinity and men. Some male survivors suffer a deep level of toxic shame, thinking they should have been "tough enough" to fight off their abuser.

Many male victims struggle terribly because they may have ejaculated during the abuse which led to confusion and a deep sense of wondering "how" or "why". This is a normal physical reaction and in no way implies consent, an invitation, a want, or that it was enjoyable. If this has happened to you, know now, you are not alone! Men assaulted when they were children or teenagers may react differently than those assaulted as adults. The following are some of the common aspects by boys and men sexually traumatized:

- Depression, eating disorders, PTSD, flashbacks, severe anxiety
- Avoidance of places and people that remind you of the abuse
- Questioning your sexual orientation
- Fearing there is no future
- Feeling like "I am less of a man"
- Feeling like you are about to break, can't sleep, can't ever feel relaxed
- Self-blame for not being able to stop yourself from having an erection or ejaculation
- Withdrawal from society and friendships
- Fear of telling anyone and being disbelieved or judged

Being sexually assaulted isn't related to the sexual orientation of the victim or the perpetrator, and in no way is someone's sexual orientation the cause of the rape. It is not a rarity for boys and men to have questions about who they are sexually after surviving the abuse, and that is completely understandable. The tremendous angst male victims experience if they had an erection or ejaculated during the abuse traumatizes the person in many ways.

Flashbacks of ejaculating during a rape plague the psyche of these boys and men. An erection and ejaculation are involuntary physiological reactions, which you have zero control over. Even worse, the perpetrators often hold the victim's physical reaction to the rape over their heads and secretly torture their victims with comments such as "You know you loved it". As much as I am scientifically writing about an erection or orgasm in no way invited the trauma or condoned a rape, I also know how hard it is to accept that truth in your very inner-self. If this is your reality, acceptance of the truth will set you free.

It can be extremely difficult for men or boys to tell someone about being sexually traumatized. The fear of being judged, or not being believed, and living with the knowledge that masculinity is a stereotype, may make it seem impossible to tell anyone, even a best friend. Men who have been sexually assaulted or raped by a woman may struggle with whether or not they are a victim. I know of cases where victims were as young as 7 or 8 years old and were abused by a female and still struggled with whether or not it was the same thing as being raped by a man. Here are some helpful tools if someone has told you about their abuse:

- Be a good listener. It is common for an individual experiencing a crisis to believe that no one can understand what happened to them. So, giving them your undivided attention will help allay their fear of being disbelieved.
- Validate their emotions and feelings by not making cliche comments such as "Time will cure it" "Worse things happen" "You'll get over it and it will get better". Make comments such as "That must have been a terrible experience" "Talk to me, I am listening" "Thank you for trusting me".
- Show concern by directly letting them know you care about them such as "I care about your feelings" "You can turn to me for support"
- Don't ask the person to go into the details of their trauma. We always feel curious about how a person was assaulted, even if it is because we want to have a better understanding. Let the victim or survivor choose how much and when they want to disclose those details with

you, and do your best to stay supportive and listen in a non-judgmental way.

- Take the time to gather appropriate resources and give them to the survivor. There are often aspects in boy's and men's lives that limit their ability to access services and other resources after a sexual trauma. Trans men may find it difficult to go to the police and black men may feel the same way. Show great sensitivity to these anxieties when working to support a victim, and take the time to gather information on where they can get help.

Intimate Partner Sexual Trauma

Most often sexual violence is committed by someone the victim knows, and this can be a boyfriend, girlfriend, husband, or wife (any intimate partner). There are varying terms for this type of abuse including spousal rape, domestic violence, intimate partner rape, and marital rape. It really doesn't matter how the term is coined; rape is rape! Rarely is rape by someone close to the victim a one-time event. It usually starts with the perp exhibiting controlling behaviors that eventually turn into verbal, physical, and sexual abuse.

If you are being assaulted sexually by someone you are in a relationship with, it can be very scary to come forward. You may worry about where you can go, the safety of your children, how your family is going to react, may even still love your abuser, and feel confused about whether or not you have been raped or abused. It is completely understandable, these feelings! The following are some warning signs to watch out for if you know of someone or if your partner begins to do:

1. Starts trying to cut you off from friends and family
2. Acts extremely upset or jealous about you going anywhere without them

3. Insults you repeatedly and then apologizes
4. Starts to interfere with you going to work or school
5. Tries to make your decisions for you
6. Starts to destroy your things or threatens to hurt your pets, or get rid of your pets (believe it or not, this is not uncommon).
7. Threatens to have your children taken away or begins to verbally abuse your children
8. Tells you that you are worthless and unlovable.
9. Takes control of your money and finances

Drug-Facilitated Sexual Trauma

Victims who were drugged and then assaulted tend to blame themselves. Being drunk or high doesn't give someone an excuse to rape or abuse you and it doesn't make it your fault when they do! Drug-Facilitated rape happens when drugs or alcohol have been used to manipulate someone's ability to provide consent. Perpetrators prey upon victims when their inhibitions are lowered, or their ability to resist is compromised, as well as their ability to recall the details of the assault. One of the more common methods you have probably heard of is "date rape drugs" such as "roofies" or "GHB", however, alcohol is the most commonly used substance to facilitate drug-induced assaults. It can be anybody, even someone you could never imagine doing such a thing, like someone you have known for years, and you would have never believed they would take advantage of you, until the one time you were highly intoxicated, maybe even passed-out, and it happened.

I was listening to a fellow survivor talk about being raped. He said he weighed 225 lbs. and stood 6'3. He said he never thought there was anywhere he couldn't go that he would have to worry about this. In his case, someone slipped Xanax into his drink at a club and he ended up in some hotel, with only a vague memory of the assault. He never gave consent and was deeply traumatized. It took him years to come forward. When it affected his life to the point of it becoming unmanageable, he finally asked for help.

Drug-facilitated sexual violence can happen when the victim has voluntarily been consuming too much alcohol or drugs, or when the perpetrator forces the victim to consume the substance by giving it to them without their knowledge. College students can be at high risk for drug-facilitated sexual abuse. It can happen in a variety of ways:

- Pressuring or coercing a person to drink more, smoke more pot, ingest more drugs than they wanted to.
- Refusing or ignoring a person who is overly intoxicated and needs help.
- Intentionally waiting for a person to become intoxicated enough that they are less likely to be able to resist.
- Not telling someone they have been drugged

The following are some of the substances sexual perpetrators use to make a victim incapacitated:

- Most commonly used is alcohol
- Benzodiazepines such as Xanax, Valium, Ativan, Klonopin, and others
- Muscle relaxers such as Soma or Flexeril
- Sleeping aids such as Unisom or Benadryl
- Street or designer drugs such as Rohypnol (roofies), ecstasy (X), ketamine (Special K), which can be slipped into a beverage without changing the taste, odor, or color of the drink.

Many victims strongly believe it is their fault after being drug-induced and sexually assaulted. I remember a girl telling me she was hooked on Cocaine and suffered a brutal rape, and her family told her "What do you expect is going to happen if you put yourself in a dangerous atmosphere" "You might as well have held up a sign saying 'please rape me', you might as well keep it to yourself because it is really your fault for being there". She said other people told her she was asking for it by going to a high-risk area to buy drugs. This is so sad to me because no one deserves to be violated.

People struggling with addiction are targeted by sexual predators because they know the chances of them getting arrested are slim to none. Someone can choose to drink too much, that doesn't mean they have chosen to be raped. Knowing the warning signs of being drugged can help you to turn immediately to someone you can trust. Here are some of the signs that you may have or someone you know may have been drugged :

- Short of breath
- Feeling drunk after one drink or no alcohol
- Loss of bladder or bowel control
- Nausea
- Suddenly shaking, feeling cold, or sweating
- Dizziness, blurred vision, or feeling disoriented
- Waking up in a strange place or not remembering how you got home

If you think you may have been drugged, rush yourself to a hospital, if you can't go immediately, save some urine in a cup, seal it and put it in the refrigerator, and call the National Sexual Assault Hotline at 800.656.HOPE (4673) to find a medical facility or hospital that can give you a forensic sexual assault exam and test your urine and blood for substances.

Incest

Few topics in psychology elicit a more visceral, profound, and polarized reaction than those related to incestual behaviors which are a violation of the most guarded and sacred taboos in society. The painful, complex, and clinical challenges of the incest victim presented to healthcare specialists create one of the most troublesome clinical dilemmas in the helping industry. The close relationship between the abuser and the victim complicates incestuous trauma because it is both betrayal trauma and relational trauma. Relational trauma results in a significant lack of trust in other people and increased confusion, hurt, and anger about what a family is in general. These victims do not have the belief in family safety, which results in a negative self-evaluation.

Betrayal trauma entails the unique pain that comes with being violated by the person or people who have a duty and obligation to nurture and protect the victim (Clancy, 2009). Furthermore, those same people whose duty it is to protect children, juveniles, teens, and young adults, who don't believe or offer to help, add to the betrayal trauma. The threat to the relationship can be so profound that the victim may feel compelled to disclaim the experienced betrayal.

Incest can lead to a condition called traumatic bonding, which is a type of relational trauma. Traumatic bonding happens when the perpetrator abuses the victim in the form of humiliations, intimidation, harassment, or beatings, while at the same time, shows some form of affection, attention, and connectedness. The victim forms a trauma bond that links the abuse to a bizarre form of caring. The awful reality is that often once the incest is finally exposed, the victim experiences repeated traumatization due to the family's rejection and even watching them take the perpetrator's side. Authorities can act very insensitively toward the victim, showering them with doubt about their claim being true, and wanting to avoid the long and drawn-out process of investigating the claim, which quite often, the rest of the family denies. My research identified some of the categories of incest including:

- Affection-based incest: The abuser emphasizes how special

the relationship is, but only in a sexual manner, otherwise nurture is neglected as well as affection, so it is the only provision for closeness.

- Erotic-based incest: In this case, more than one victim is involved and more than one perpetrator. It is a chaotic sexual atmosphere.
- Violence-based incest: The abuser commits sexualized anger on the victim, and usually conducts physical harm during the rape.
- Rage-based incest: The abuser is sadistic and is of grave danger to the victim.

It is imperative to know that if you have been sexually abused by a family member that you are not alone and that it is not your fault. Over 35% of juvenile and child sexual assault victims are perpetrated by a family member, according to the Department of Justice (2019). Incest happens when a family member forces unwanted sex on another family member. Victims and survivors of incest have an extremely hard time disclosing a rape from a family member. They may love their abuser or be afraid of what the abuser will do to them if they tell. Fearing no one will believe them often makes the incest victim hesitant to tell.

Commonly, incest victims have spoken out, and the abuse has been ignored, where the family walks around like nothing is happening. Sometimes, the abuser has told the victim that it is normal and happens in every family. Incest victims often do not know there is available help or anyone they can trust. Most of all they fear losing their families or being punished for telling.

Rape Trauma Syndrome

Rape is so devastating that it elicits a wide range of physical and emotional consequences immediately following the attack. The incident may be so powerful that it leaves the victim in a state of disbelief and shock. As the shock starts to dissipate the victim is left in a desperate state of fear of death, injury, mutilation, degradation, embarrassment, rage, self-blame, humiliation, and revenge. The broad range of emotions gives rise to rapid mood swings. The victim struggles to express themselves by being tense, sobbing, and visibly restless when trying to specifically describe the details of the attack.

While seemingly controlled, the victim may hide or mask their feelings and come off as calm, subdued, and composed. Physically, the victim is usually sore all over their body with concentrated pain in the areas of the body that were zeroed in upon, such as the vagina and rectum. Rectal bleeding may persist for days. When forced to commit oral sex, the victims may have injured teeth, gums, cheeks, and throat. Trouble sleeping plagues rape victims, especially those who were attacked during their hours of slumber. These victims may awaken screaming each night at the same time that their attack took place.

Eating patterns and a diminished appetite also occur in many cases for rape victims. Nausea overwhelms many rape survivors and therefore, females should rule out pregnancy. Fear can overcome the life of a rape victim and confusion, problems with decision making, and emotional fatigue are among the impairments associated with the trauma of rape. There is a vast inability to absorb new information and the rape victim may scramble to change their location, phone number, even their place of employment. During the acute phase, from a few days to a month, emotional vulnerability is present, so crisis intervention is imperative.

The Underground Stage of Rape Trauma Syndrome

The underground stage is when the rape victim tries to go back to their life as if the rape never happened. During this phase, the victim blocks out all memories and thoughts about the rape from their minds and doesn't even want to talk about it. They unrealistically want to forget it ever happened and then they slowly lose the ability to concentrate and slip into a depression. Unfortunately, some victims stay in the underground stage for years, and people may think the victim has learned how to cope with the trauma or maybe even has gotten over it. The most common action during this phase is avoidance, where the victim steers clear of any themes common to the rape. Here lies unresolved trauma and avoidance is the only coping mechanism the survivor knows how to employ.

The Reorganization Stage of Rape Trauma Syndrome

Reorganization is the long-term process where the victim starts to return to the initial stage of turmoil experienced in the acute phase. Nightmares, certain smells, court dates, possibly seeing their assailant again, may trigger this stage of the Syndrome. If the individual is a victim of childhood sexual trauma, this phase is magnified by emotions connected to those events. It can be horrifically frightening to enter back into the acute phase, and the person can find themselves shocked with emotional pain.

Phobia and other fears may develop, either specifically related to the appearance of their attacker or to the circumstances that surrounded the initial attack. Fantasies of violent revenge can consume the victim, understandably so. Sleeping and eating disturbances may come back, but despite these intense difficulties, it is important for everyone involved to understand that this is a normal part of the integrating process of reorganizing their life that was so violently disrupted. If the offender was a stranger, fear seems to be the predominant obstacle to recovery. Factors that can influence the reorganization phase include:

- The age or developmental stage of the victim
- Support network
- Cultural background
- The nature of the attack

- The relationship with the attacker
- The degree and type of force or violence

Developmental Phase of Rape Trauma Syndrome

The developmental phase of the Rape Trauma Syndrome is very important to understand both in the way the survivor expresses their emotions and what the attack meant to them. The phase is also determined by the victim's level of emotional and community support. You can never assume to know what rape means to different people. For instance, some child victims are more seriously injured by the betrayal than the act; for a teen, their sexuality may differ, and for an adult as with every other age, PTSD. During this phase issues of control, power, independence, and trust may fluctuate between more and less depending on the age of the victim.

For a teen, for instance, the family's reaction is of great importance because the assault interfered with their growing need for support because the assault is often in conflict with their developmental need for independence. The developmental stage of the victim also impacts the way they express their feelings. Adolescents may giggle inappropriately causing adults to think they are not that bothered by the trauma. Older adults may become dependent on their children and lose their ability to live independently.

How families, friends, communities, and institutions react to a rape victim is an extremely important aspect of recovery. Families are either supportive or harmful, there is no in-between. It is only natural to want to be overprotective of a loved one traumatized by rape. If the victim is met with disbelief or their cries go unheard, the potential for healing is greatly impaired. If the family and other people significant to the victim's life are unwilling or unable to help, the victim must find help elsewhere. Also, learning everything possible about the victim's cultural background is a must if you want to help a victim. Some cultures cast off women who have been raped because they are no longer virgins. It is not anyone's

place to judge another's cultural belief system, but it helps t
educate yourself on the matter so you can be of the utmost help t
the victim. You never know when you may be the person
coworker, neighbor, or friend turns to after being raped.

Slut-Shaming

Slut-shaming is a type of bullying, often on the Internet (cyberbu
lying) where females are humiliated and degraded for being sexu
ally active or presumably sexually active. Girls are often ridicule
for the clothes they wear or just the way they look. According t
the American Association of University Women (AAUM, 2011),
rd. of all students from 6-12th grade experience unwelcome
sexual gestures, comments, jokes, or textual comments about then
Furthermore, slut-shaming is now considered a common metho
of sexual harassment the middle and high school-age children a
faced with today.

While there are different types of slut-shaming, perpetrators sha
explicit images and videos of girls and boys they are targetir
along with lewd comments, often without the victim's knowledg
that they were ever taken. Sometimes, the photos are doctored ar
pictures of young people's faces are placed on illicit photos
someone else's body. Body shaming is usually part of the bully
M.O. Bullies have taken to Instagram with a young lady's cleavag
showing with rude captions under the pictures.

Sometimes, young people videotape their sexual acts witho
telling their partners and then post them on social media! Wh
these young people may not be aware of is that these activities a
against the law. Child pornography charges can be filed agair
whoever took the video or pictures and anyone else that copied t
pictures or video. If caught with such pics or videos on a c
phone, possession of child pornography charges can be file
Sexting is also an avenue for slut-shaming. For example, you m
trust someone you are involved with enough to send them se

pictures or texts and they can then be used against you at a later time. This is also unlawful and can result in child pornography charges. It is extremely important to educate children on the negative consequences and personal damage caused by slut-shaming.

Very much like rape culture, we are now faced with a slut-shaming culture. Schools can mistakenly play a role in the slut-shaming culture by enforcing dress codes, which in effect sends a message that girls will be punished for the type of clothes they wear because they are destructive to the boys. This is a slippery slope because of the implication that females are to blame for slut-shaming, pretty much like victim-blaming. It also implies that young men cannot control their behaviors.

Many people see slut-shaming as a double standard, where males receive adoration and praise for their sexual activities and females are branded as trashy, loose, a slut, whore, skank, and these are just a few of the awful names I came across while researching the subject. However, I did see several instances where males were ridiculed, as well. Whoever this happens to is left with a deep sense of shame, humiliation, embarrassment, and pain.

Feelings of low self-worth and hopelessness can complicate the lives of these victims, as well as bullying themselves, eating disorders, and sleep issues. For a young person who already suffers from body-image issues, slut-shaming can push them over the edge and possibly lead to suicidal ideation or worse, suicide (AAUM, 2011). Parents and school officials can prevent slut-shaming by talking to the kids about sexual trauma, sexual harassment, and the risks associated with such crimes.

FOUR

Regaining Healthy Sexuality

Undoubtedly, surviving sexual trauma impacts an individual's view of their future sex life, even if they are in a secure, and healthy relationship, and sexually active. Survivors of sexual trauma may question how to enjoy healthy intimacy and sex when traumatic memories can trigger confusion and terror. By now you hopefully know for a fact it wasn't your fault if you are a survivor of sexual violence. No matter what pain or shame you have had to endure, you can move forward and heal to find healthy sex and love.

At this point, it has been well established the difference between abuse and sex, as well as understanding consent. Now that you know the difference, you can begin to acknowledge how your desire for healthy intimacy is nothing close to that terror that forced you into submission. With consent, sex is what you want! If you face unwanted arousal during abuse, you know it wasn't a choice. It was just human physiology without any pleasure. Wanting to and having sex is a decision you consciously make in your brain, something you want to do out of your own free will, and something you look forward to enjoying.

Healthy sexual activities include:

- Your consent
- Your own free will
- It is enjoyable, likable, and pleasurable

Sexual trauma can trigger intense negative feelings connected to sexual desire for survivors. Scary things trigger the brain's fight/flight/freeze response, which you cannot control. Deciding you want to have a healthy sex life lies in feeling self-love, compassion, and self-care. Survivors commonly avoid emotions about the traumatic memories and the abuse so they can function on a daily basis. The trouble caused here is that pushing the bad experience deeper into your psyche, will eventually surface in the form of an illness. Unresolved anger, shame, guilt, and resentments are perfect ingredients for mental illness.

Talking about the trauma is the only real way you can recover and begin to live a normal life. Antidepressants may be prescribed, along with meditation, but talk therapy actually works wonders. It is imperative that you find a treatment team that specializes in trauma therapy, a place where you can verbalize your pain and grief and start to process what happened during that horrible time in your life.

I want to empower you to understand that you absolutely have the capability of processing the past trauma and find a fulfilling life that includes healthy sex! One of the best methods for beginning the recovery process is finding a good trauma therapist. There are all sorts of therapists out there and all sorts of therapy, but trauma victims need trauma-focused protocols that are specifically focused on treating people who unfortunately have suffered sexual violence. The emotional and spiritual trauma can affect your life years after the event and it is an issue that is not easily laid to rest, especially if trying to do it alone.

The Body Knows

Survivors of sexual trauma who are healing have to recover from specific physical feelings that have kept them from feeling at home in their own bodies. For a long time, I felt disconnected from my body, so it was really hard to feel connected to someone else's body. Many victims of sexual violence body's freeze at the mere thought of intimacy or they might not feel safe. When this is the case, it is very hard to feel pleasure while having sex.

When you don't feel okay in your own body, it blocks the intimate sensual pleasures that make sex so enjoyable. It is a powerful defense mechanism developed over time to protect you, so don't even hate that part of yourself. Just knowing about it helps. The problem is that if you don't relearn how to process what happened to you, this defense mechanism keeps you from feeling fully alive. Another common interference with a survivor's sex life is that the trauma may have left them feeling undeserving of pleasure. The traumatic stress severely affects the survivor's self-worth and confidence levels, which society further perpetuates. So, you blaming you, and society blaming you, creates a never-ending cycle of toxic shame. This spreads out to every area of your life, which without help will leave you thinking you will never be able to experience sexual pleasure because your needs don't matter; NOT TRUE!

I also want to point out that most survivors experience various other traumatic events other than the sexual ones. Verbal, mental, and physical abuse, on top of the sexual abuse, also interferes with your ability to enjoy sex, as it compounds the feelings of disconnectedness and fear.

If you are relating to this, I am sorry. No human being in the world deserves to be put through the pain and lifelong effects of sexual abuse. Know there is help and support, and that there are ways that you can reclaim your life and experience joy and pleasure your sex life. I did not say again, because, for many survivors, the have never enjoyed sex, not for a moment in their life. Sexual violence gets stored in your nervous system where it forms patterns that seem uncomfortably foreign to you and keeps you from knowing your true self. Therefore, in order to have a healthy sex life post-trauma, you have to work with your nervous system so you can rejoin your body. Here are some techniques to do so:

Talk therapy helps individuals overcome the pain and duress, along with the dysfunctional lifestyle that accompanies sex abuse. Cognitive behavioral therapy, as previously discussed, actually changes the way your brain responds to traumatic memories, toxic shame, and self-loathing that many victims of sexual assault encounter. Our brains have neuroplasticity which means they are malleable. The chemical and neurological pathways in our brains can change and mold with time. This concept is extremely important to understand for those who have experienced severe trauma, such as childhood sexual abuse or rape. With the right tools, the brain can be altered in positive ways post-trauma. According to scientific researchers Su, Veeravagu, and Grant (2016), there are three separate neuroplasticity phases that occur after a person experiences trauma:

Immediately after: Neurons in the brain start to die and certain pathways are decreased, severely changing the way the mind responds. This phase lasts about two days, and secondary pathways are uncovered which may never have been used. Within a week, new neurons with synapses, and other cells begin to replace the dead ones and the healing process has begun. The brain is changed forever from the trauma but within a few weeks, new cells keep getting generated and new pathways begin to open up. This is the most critical time for healing to occur from trauma. You can train these new pathways and remap your brain chemistry with the help of therapy, and sometimes medication. If you know someone or you yourself have recently been assaulted you can reclaim your life with trauma-focused therapy.

What Is Trauma-Focused Therapy?

Trauma-focused therapy is conducted by professionals who are educated and have experience treating victims of sexual violence. Trauma happens when your mind cannot cope with an obnoxious event. Some therapists may want to use CBT and other psychotherapy, but an eclectic approach using multiple therapeutic tools, I find work the best. The victim has to prepare their brain for the trauma work at hand before they start therapy. You should be looking forward to achieving recovery and healing from the past, but it is by no means an easy path. Acknowledging your treatment goals is very important, as well as writing down your triggers and how you react to them. It is in your story—saying that you become aware of the parts of you that need to process and heal from the abuse. Here are some of the common goals of trauma therapy:

- Handling and coping with the reality of what happened to you.
- Eliminating the trauma symptoms (fear, anxiety, depression, toxic shame, etc.).
- To change your focus from the past to the present
- To enhance your day-to-day functioning
- Regaining your personal power
- Facing any addictions head-on
- Become an expert on hereditary sexual abuse
- Relapse prevention

There is no reason to ever feel self-centered for making achievable goals for yourself and to seek the benefits of trauma therapy.

Trauma-Focused Cognitive Behavioral Therapy (TFCBT)

Trauma-focused cognitive behavioral therapy (TFCBT) works on the thoughts involved with your traumatic events for up to approx ately 30 sessions. TFCBT helps trauma victims to have a better understanding of the effect trauma has on thinking patterns. The TFCBT specialist also works with the families to teach them effective communication strategies through educating them on the effects that trauma potentially had on their family member. The trauma victim can discuss their experience, while in a safe environment. The client is taught relaxation techniques so they are more comfortable discussing their "trauma narrative".

The thinking patterns are then remapped in regards to the trauma and new and appropriate ways of expressing their feelings are developed. During the course of treatment, an extensive and intensive analysis of the victims' thoughts associated with their trauma is conducted. The client is then educated on various patterns of thought available for them to adopt and replace dysfunctional and old ways of thinking. This is a very intensive treatment and sometimes the victim may feel retraumatized from going back to specific times or places where the abuse happened.

By exposing the client to their past horror, a place opens to deal with the past in new ways. The victim ends up with a new set of coping skills and essentially a new life. This is an evidence-based therapeutic technique with documented success by the Child Welfare Information Gateway, 2018. The treatment addresses unsettling and distorted attributions and beliefs associated with trauma while providing a supportive atmosphere in which the survivor is encouraged to discuss their sexual trauma and learn new coping skills to aid them in their daily life. TFCBT combines aspects from various theories and approaches including:

- Cognitive therapy, where the goal is behavior change by addressing the survivor's distorted perceptions that create points of view which are not helpful to the client.
- Behavioral therapy, where the goal is to modify habitual reactions such as fear and anger, to fewer threatening stimuli or situations.

- Family therapy takes a look at the interactional patterns among members of the family to identify and alleviate the stressors.
- Developmental neurobiology for child victims to gain insight into the child's developing brain.

TFCBT usually lasts for approximately 30 sessions and is consid-ered to be short-term treatment. Each session lasts for about a hour, with the family and the survivor seeing the therapist sepa-rately for ½ hour each. Later in treatment, the survivor will atten sessions with family members at which time they will share the: trauma narrative (Cohen, & Mannarino, 2015). NOT EASY!! I sa it's not easy because each session is about building therapeutic tru: so you can handle going over your memories out loud. Writing an discussing your trauma narrative is gut-wrenching, but als extremely freeing, but you have to do it when you're ready. The you come up with a set of goals with your therapist, and if possibl your family, and then you practice your new set of skills in trea ment until you have them down pat and can take them home. Fc me, I learned how to talk about my trauma without feeling ar shame or fear of judgment; something I didn't think was possibl The old saying, "I felt like a ton of bricks was lifted off of n chest" rang true.

Breathwork

Breathwork is a group of techniques that work to reset yo nervous system and in effect treats the effects of your trauma fro the inside out.

Holotropic Breathwork is a powerful way to explore your innermc self and find empowerment through your inborn inner wisdo and move you toward healthy transformation and wholene: Supporting, acknowledging, and accessing your healing intelligen from the inside is the way Holotropic breathing works (Grof

Grof, 2021). It is a simple process that combines powerfully expressive music with deep breathing while in a special setting that you have designed to be your sanctuary. You just lay comfortably on a mat, play the music, and listen to your breathing until you enter a dream-like state of consciousness. Once you are in this state, the inner healing process is naturally activated, bringing you to a particular experience of peace and contentment. With your inner healing process activated you can calm the stressful content that is brought forth.

Deep breathing breathwork is a way for your body to take in more oxygen. We don't normally breathe deeply, most of us breathe in a shallow manner from the chest. By deep breathing, you take in more oxygen and expel more carbon dioxide, which resets your body, naturally, and leaves you in a calm and relaxed state. When I first learned to deep breathe, I really didn't believe it would make much of a difference in my level of anxiety. But I learned how to do it, and I kept doing it because they told me it would help. Now, I can't imagine not doing it. It just takes time and practice and eventually, you start to recognize the difference it makes in your life. Also, you can do it anytime and anywhere. You don't need a mat or music; you just use it as needed. It helps you cope with the stress of traumatic memories and it is used a great deal for veterans with PSD.

You can practice deep breathing with your eyes closed or open. It is suggested that trauma survivors leave their eyes open as it helps to keep you grounded in the present. Sometimes, I like to close my eyes, but not when I first started. It can take some practice to re-learn how to breathe. The more you practice, the easier it becomes.

1. Make yourself comfortable
2. Put one hand on your chest and one on your stomach
3. Slowly breathe in through your nose, feeling your stomach rise with your hand and count to five
4. Think about how your lungs are filling all the way up

5. Slowly breathe out, as much as you can, feeling your stomach go back down.
6. Do this ten times and return to normal breathing (I do this several times a day).

Nature Walks and Forest Bathing to Heal Trauma

Few things keep us mindful and more connected to our bodies than time in nature. Taking time to pause and stand rapt in awe can tremendously reduce stress and the symptoms of traumatization. The feeling of awe is the actual reason why nature walks are so good for us. It is the old adage of stopping to smell the roses. came across another term for nature walks, and I love it! It is called forest bathing! Connecting to nature is a powerful way to heal and incorporate into your recovery program. Walking barefoot in the sand or anywhere touching the earth heals the mind, body, and soul in infinite ways. Natural landscapes, such as the beach or the forest, expose our bodies to sunshine, healthy bacteria, and certain chemicals called phytoncides that are released from trees and have been proven to boost our immune system (Gilbert, 2020).

Nature lowers stress hormones, regulates our blood pressure and heart rate, and helps alleviate anxiety and depression, something can attest to. Forest bathing connects you to positive energies, as does any form of nature bathing. Exposing yourself to nature, like hiking, gardening, bird watching, etc., will take you on a spiritual trip towards reclaiming your life, and will enhance your sex life too. Connecting to nature reminds us of what a healthy relationship means as it represents the land and those who live on it. It encourages self-reconciliation.

The flexibility that nature walks offer makes it the perfect activity for trauma survivors. Make your relationship with nature personal. This is one area of your life where there are no rules, except for no littering. If you don't feel like walking, just stand there and find the awe in something you see, feel, hear, taste, or touch. It can be you ay to meditate or exercise and it will help you to adopt an attitude f gratitude.

ind yourself the biggest tree trunk around and make it a place here you feel like you belong. Choose a tree with the qualities you dmire such as confidence, security, and strength, and notice how ealthy its boundaries are in reference to the other trees as if it ould clearly speak its mind! Lean against the tree and notice its rength, and safety, as it won't let you fall. Meditate on how you an absorb the qualities of nature as you lean against the tree. llow your tree to comfort and strengthen you, and provide you ith resilience as you continue to bask in the positive and onderful qualities of your tree.

Eye Movement Desensitization and Reprocessing (EMDR)

ye Movement Desensitization and Reprocessing, or EMDR, is a erapeutic technique that has been successfully demonstrated to eat victims of sexual violence (Babbel, 2013). EMDR works well ith TFCBT to bring quick and lasting solace from trauma associ- ed with sexual abuse. We are abused sexually, we have trauma, d then our brains get so overwhelmed that we experience trau- atic stress which turns into a lifelong battle with anxiety, depres- on, toxic shame, and all of the other previously discussed mptoms of rape.

ith EMDR, the brain reprocesses the information connected to e trauma until it is no longer emotionally disturbing and disrup- e to our lives. The survivor performs eye movements, laterally ile at the same time, thinking about the various parts of the umatic memory. Moving your eyes from side to side or listening a beep from side to side (alternating ears) causes a change in the ain's circuitry and helps to understand and integrate our memo- s within the bigger picture of our overall life experiences.

EMDR also helps us understand our own unique potential. More than teaching us how to reprocess those awful events of our past, it helps us to see how false beliefs we have about ourselves are limiting us. Thoughts like "I'm not enough" "I don't deserve to be happy" and then help us to let go of those negative thoughts. This technique moves the victim through the past trauma and not around it, but also helps change our self-perceptions, ultimately making a huge change for the better in our lives.

Winning the Battle Within

Some survivors choose to speak to someone kind with whom they are close to about how they are feeling, while others choose to remain private about their experience. Whichever you choose talking about it can help you to feel less isolated. Many institutions offer group meetings and crisis intervention, but at least try to talk just in general at first, to avoid re-traumatization. Processing through shame and guilt can be an intense experience so it can be helpful to start out writing about it first.

By identifying these feelings, you can begin to work through them rather than carrying them around with you and into your future. is too common, the self-blame, I know it is. That broken record playing over and over again, that you could have or should have done something differently. It is normal to be afraid of feeling sexual pleasure as disconnecting from your body as a means of survival. But, feeling afraid and numb to your own sensations is like staying trapped in the sordid details of the trauma.

It is sad but true that a lot of people, including survivors, don't always know the facts about sexual violence. For many victims, it was the norm and something to survive, even though the responsibility always falls on the offender, never the victim, maybe you didn't know that when it was happening and now it feels burned into your soul that you are somehow to blame. When society wrongfully blames a victim of sexual violence for what happened them, it leads to the victim also blaming themselves. I realized this and came to understand that it was up to me to help inform society and other survivors, along with anyone that will help me, what happens to a person who has been traumatized or abused sexually.

I want to spread the facts about sexual violence so people will challenge common beliefs about sexual assault and rape. These myths allow the abuser to move about freely in society, by victim-blaming. For instance, most victims of sexual assault don't have injuries to their private parts or other parts of their body that can be seen. Then people question if it really happened because they do not see blood and bruises. The deepest and most common and severe injuries are emotional and psychological and can ruin a person's life.

It takes time to recover from sexual violence, so it is very important to practice self-care and to accept help from others. When you feel ready, talk to groups of survivors, keeping all of the feelings in will make you sick. Find ways to spend time with supportive people, there are more of them than you realize. It is a good way to remind yourself that you are a survivor, you are alive. Write down one single achievement every day "I read a poem" "I smiled at a stranger".

Positive self-dialog is a way to lift yourself out of feeling down. Tell yourself things like "I am making it" "I will be okay". Try to use tried and true ways that helped you in the past through the tough times. If walking or listening to music makes you feel better, do more of it. Avoid drowning your sorrows in the bottom of a liquor bottle or zoning out with your third joint of the day. When it wears off you will feel much worse. Steer clear of triggers, and process them with a trauma specialist or share about them at a survivors' meeting. Take the time to nourish yourself with love and affection. Get some plants to take care of and watch them grow with your recovery. Eat healthily; your physical health affects your mental health. Any type of movement helps you become more aware of your body and can help ground you. Feeling yourself is an act of mindfulness and will help you stay rooted in the present. And PLAY! Do something enjoyable and playful.

MAP: Mental and Physical Meditation Training for Survivors of Sexual Violence

Harnessing the dual strength of exercise and meditation is key to reprogramming your brain's association with sexual trauma. When you meditate, your heartbeat and breathing slow down, and your body enters a state of lowered stress. Most people's minds wander through memories, but for victims of sexual violence, those memories are not a safe place within which to travel. Normally, these memories are mentally, physically, emotionally, and spiritually agonizing, but when you are in a lowered stress state, the memory doesn't elicit as powerful of a stress reaction.

The more you practice remembering while you are in a meditative state, the more the memory will be connected to a relaxed state, again is brain training. The process is known as exposure or extinction therapy because you are exposing yourself to the memories while staying calm and eventually, they will become extinct.

Now, if you combine the meditative state with working up a sweat, meaning exercising right after you meditate, oxygen and blood flow increase to the brain which will help to boost the reprogramming faster and stronger! Makes sense! It is a fairly simple program; you just sit and meditate for twenty minutes (using one of the breathing exercises previously described in this chapter) and then slowly walk for ten minutes.

After walking for ten minutes, do twenty minutes of aerobic exercise; get that blood pumping and work up a sweat and get those memories integrated with a healthier you. Try your best to do this twice per week, and you will probably feel better right away, but the proof will hit you after about six weeks of training. This is your first

enchmark, after which, if you keep the training up, you will reap
s benefits long-term.

Developing a Positive Sexual Self

When it comes to our youth, developing a "sex-positive" method to
sex education can help young people develop positive self-esteem,
personal values, communication skills, and responsible decision-
making abilities. For adult survivors, having been sexually abused is
not an automatic sentence to uncomfortable sexuality. Untangling
sex issues can be very tricky for a trauma survivor. First off, it is
good to remember that developing, negotiating, and maintaining a
healthy sex life is challenging for any relationship. In all relationships, partners have to learn what is sensitive, pleasurable, sensual,
joyful, and fulfilling for both people involved.

When one or both of the partners has been victimized sexually, the
couple must learn about each other in a way that feels safe and can
be mutually satisfying. Disentangling what might be impacting on
shared pleasure in sexual intimacy can be tricky. Given that sexual
abuse can have such a profound impact on people's lives, it is not
surprising that when difficulties do appear, couples can focus on the
legacy of the abuse as the source of the problem, when there might
be other factors at play.

Yes, a bit of work is required. Here are some building blocks to get
you started:

- Accurate and up-to-date knowledge about sex, your own
  sexuality, and your partner's sexuality.
- Develop the relationship around fun, love, arousal,
  lust...pleasure, not performance.
- Have the type of relationship in which good sex can
  blossom.
- Learn how to communicate non-verbally and verbally
  about sex.

- Learn to be assertive about what you want, be able to fully focus on your own pleasure.
- Learn to be sensitive to your partner's needs and how they want you to respond to them sexually.
- Appreciate the differences with understanding and acceptance of one another.

For couples, it is helpful to have an awareness about it not being uncommon for difficulties to arise and possibly memories re-appear while having sex. Circumstances are bound to replicate abuse, by accident, at some point during a sexual encounter. By talking to each other about the areas of the body that are sensitive trigger points, and scenarios that are triggers, you both can overcome these challenges and have a fulfilling sex life.

Certain positions such as doggy style, places, sounds, and smell can be agreed upon as off-limits forever or until the traumatic response to them has been eradicated. Emphasize the importance of moving slowly when developing an understanding of choice and preferences. Most importantly, get comfortable with your own body. Anyone can love sex when it's the right type of way and feelings involved. Just because someone loves sex doesn't make them a sex addict, freak, pervert, or not capable of loving you for more reasons than one. I express my feelings about touch to a person at the beginning of any relationship because I want someone to understand that I am very active and love to be touched.

Masturbation

Pleasing yourself by masturbating involves exploring your own body. Rubbing and touching parts of your body for sexual pleasure can be done alone or with your partner (mutual masturbation), long as you both agree it to be mutually enjoyable. It is a common human activity in all ages and genders. It is a healthy method for exploring the best way to reach an orgasm. It is perfectly normal masturbate as much as you want as long as it doesn't interfere with having a balanced and healthy life. Masturbation is a wonderful tool for getting back in touch with yourself, sexually in a safe place.

Creating body awareness can be thought of in the same fashion as paying attention to being tired or hungry. If you leave feeling satisfied with your partner, you may not know the best way to find pleasure for yourself or how your body reacts to different styles of stimulation and touch. Masturbation can be as regular as other forms of exercise, such as swimming or other ways you make yourself feel good, such as feeling the sun on your face or getting a massage. If you are not masturbating due to trauma, start out slowly by exploring yourself with sexual touch, work out what feels the best and what might be a trigger. It will help you understand what parts of you need to be healed and then you will be able to communicate that to your partner.

Practice masturbating at a time and place where you won't be disturbed, and treat it with kindness not as an act of labor. It is not the type of thing you have to hurry up and get it over with. You can bring back to life parts of you that feel disconnected, dead, or frozen. There is no need to rush and can be part of your meditation to feel connected to your body. The frequency of masturbation is different and unique to each person. Some individuals feel a sense of shame or guilt about masturbating because of religious, cultural, or spiritual beliefs. It is not immoral nor wrong, but you still may hear societal messages that it is dirty or shameful. If you feel guilty about masturbating, talk to your therapist or someone you can trust that will help you to move past the shame or guilt.

Some of the health benefits to masturbation include:

- By exploring your sexuality alone, you can also release sexual tension.
- It can help you to familiarize yourself with how you

respond sexually, which can then be communicated to a partner.
- It definitely helps you to relax.
- Helps you sleep better.
- Releases feel-good endorphins
- Enhances body image and self-esteem

Myths about Masturbation

- Makes you infertile
- Causes blindness
- Makes you go crazy
- It's perverted
- Lowers your libido

FIVE

Being Free and Breaking Away from Depression

One of the hardest parts of breaking away from depression is that the depression itself is what gets in the way of its recovery. The more depressed I felt, the harder it was to get up and do something about it. When my symptoms were mild, I didn't have a hard time calling my therapist or taking a walk, but when they were bad just picking up the phone seemed like a monumental task. About five years ago, I was coping with a very difficult episode of depression. I spent endless days not doing very much at all, except for going to work.

I knew from my past episodes that I needed to start focusing on my recovery. I should have immediately called my therapist, started jogging, or tapping into my spiritual self. Mostly, I knew I had to stay out of the bed. The more I tried to stay away from laying down the more my couch was calling my name. It seemed like I would have to climb a mountain in order to feel even a little bit better, so instead, I stayed depressed.

The desire for sex comes from the brain, and the genitals rely on brain chemicals to stimulate arousal, as well as pumping extra blood to the places that need it in order to have sex. When you're depressed, the brain's chemical flow is disrupted making "doing it" much more difficult. Not only that, but antidepressants can also have negative effects on your sex life. With each day, I felt worse because I wasn't participating in the solution, I was staying in the problem. Then I started getting down on myself for not doing much, and of course, that made it worse.

Depression and being a survivor can cause problems in your sex life, but there is help for resolving both problems. Just treating the sex problem or just treating the depression doesn't fix both issues. Don't stop taking any medications without the doctor's advice. I got some good advice when I finally asked for it, and that advice was to take one tiny step per day. Like taking a pill only it was just to take a step, only one small step each day in the right direction.

I started out by just making one phone call a day to another survivor, and just saying "Hi, I am just calling you to just make the call so I can be doing something to help myself out of this depression." To my surprise every time I made that call, people immediately understood, wished me luck, and didn't try to keep me on the phone! So, my "zero-done" day turned into a one-thing done day and so on. Just committing to one small thing each day gave me an achievable goal. I wasn't about to turn my whole life around with just that one thing, but I was on my way to getting better.

One of the main symptoms of depression is being unable to enjoy those things you normally love to do, like sex. Individuals suffering from depression generally don't feel good about themselves, and sometimes can view being with their partner in a negative way which impacts their sexual desire. A loss of appetite both with sex and food, added to the sadness, lowered energy, and emotional fatigue is predominant feelings someone has when they are depressed. The good news is that being in a sexual slump related to your depression is usually temporary, so don't think the rest of your life is going to be sexless.

For the longest time as someone subjected to the situation at hand, I felt trapped, within myself to the point I couldn't trust anyone since the trauma happened in my childhood. As I got older, I felt lost, like Tom Hanks in the movie Castaway. But throughout time and growing, I found the only way to release myself from depression, anxiety, self-abuse, narcissism, etc., was to talk about it to the ones closest to me. It was hard because I didn't know if the reaction was going to be good or bad from the ones closest to me! It took time but like people say "time heals all" just gotta learn how to heal it yourself and the rest will fall in place! Those baby steps I was taking started the tide turning. Instead of my depression growing stronger, I started to slightly feel better. That led to doing two achievable goals per day, which was another milestone in my recovery.

Coping with Nightmares and Flashbacks

Flashbacks are like having a real nightmare while you are wide awake. They take you right back to that dangerous place again as if you are really there. They come out of nowhere and are very scary. Many things can trigger a flashback: a time of night, day, year; certain smells (for me it was hand lotion), certain people, pictures, and unfortunately having sex. They are memories that are yet to be processed because they are so stressful. It is completely normal to want and push these flashbacks/memories away. However, they remain unresolved and that only makes them stronger in the future.

Here are some methods I use to cope with flashbacks and hopefully they will help you too if you are experiencing the same:

- Stop whatever it is you are doing at that moment
- Change something in your environment and deep breathe (I go and grab an ice cube if I can and it immediately grounds me and stops the flashback, I concentrate on how cold it is and how it starts melting in my hand, or I will drink something warm such as my

favorite tea and concentrate on the warmth and sweetness in my mouth).

- Move yourself to a more comfortable and safe feeling place. Maybe you have to walk out to your car, or the patio or if you are at work, create a place just for this purpose.
- Call your support network
- Process the flashback on a piece of paper (this can be painful but it will also help to release it from your emotions to a physical means of resolution).
- Remind yourself that flashbacks are part of your condition and they are a normal response to what happened to you.

FLASHBACK HALTING TOOL

Right now, I am emotionally experiencing_____

Right now, in my body I am sensing_____

Right now, is the Date_____Time_____Place_____

Right now, around me I can see_____

So, I know (write down your trauma) isn't happening right now_____

One Day at a Time

When fighting depression, it is important to honestly take thin one day at a time (one of AA's slogans). This is an actual skill th requires living in the moment. Spending time in the past and in th future X's out today. Living one day at a time entails getting u each morning and recommitting yourself to recovery, literally on daily basis. This means whatever life throws at you, and regardle of the past, you are making a conscious decision to remain recovery, just for today. Sometimes this means that even on difficu days, when your motivation and hopes are at a low point, that you do something in the way of practicing self-care. Falling back on accomplishing one small thing and making it a non-zero day, can change everything.

Going back to just having a non-zero day as your goal shows you that you have tools to pick yourself up during tough times, so you don't ever have to face your lowest low again, just by going back to doing one small thing. Even if it is after working your way up to accomplishing many goals per day when the tough times come a-knockin ' you have an opportunity to prove to yourself that you can be held accountable for your recovery. Making that unspoken promise to yourself gives you your daily intention to make it through days that are more difficult than others.

Part of the purpose behind one day at a time is that it keeps you in the present rather than the past, which is one of the greatest tools recovery offers. Mindfulness or staying in the moment, has been a practiced skill for thousands of years by spiritual leaders as a method of experiencing God or a power higher than themselves. Staying present or living one day at a time means quelling your regrets and resentments and not fearing your future, but rather finding peace in this very moment in time in recovery. Focusing on the trauma, when you are not in therapy, leads to excessive anxiety, does anxiety about what is going to happen tomorrow.

Guilt and shame are the fastest way to fall back into severe depression. So, do one small thing and go get yourself an ice cream cone. By tossing aside all anxiety that is not concerned with today, you can give your attention to what you can control. It reminds me of Scarlett O'Hara (Vivien Leigh) in "Gone with The Wind", she said, "I won't think about that today — I'll think about that tomorrow".

Creating Your Own Lane

"For my thoughts are not your thoughts,

> **neither are your ways my ways, saith the Lord."**
>
> Isaiah 55:8

Creating my own lane was a breakthrough for me in my recovery. I had to stop worrying about how other people were getting things done and doing their things, and simply practice some self honesty and figure out who I really am and what makes me unique. When a person creates their own path, it helps to regain and connect one's mind, body, and soul with itself. By creating your own lane people will take notice of your actions good, and bad. Those who have done wrong by you will eventually remove themselves from your life because they can't "cross over into your lane" so to speak! "Creating your lane" brings respect, confidence, love, happiness, and structure to rebuilding yourself. T.R.U.T.H. also will help as well (Talk, Real, Understanding, Truth, Hurts).

So, I had to ask myself some tough questions:

- The first question was "what is my zone of brilliance?" Here you want to be as detailed as you can. "I am really good at ..." "I am a genius when it comes to ..."
- What sets me apart from everyone else? Here you figure out what experiences make you unique. What do you have to offer this world?
- What is my recovery process? What tools are specifically designed for my life? From what angle do I want to approach the world?
- What are my passions?
- Who am I as a human being? What about me do my friends and family like? Am I kind and empathetic? Do I have a good sense of humor? Do I value myself? Am I honest?

- Most of all, don't be tempted to jump back into the fast lane!

These days, I am trying to live my best life, and this is what I want for you. To be the best version of yourself, to be a decent human being, in general, staying in your own lane is a master skill! Recently my friend found himself in a situation where he was, well for lack of a better word, gossiping. He ended up in a yelling match with a friend of his over some random statement. He was disappointed in himself, as he shared with me, for several reasons. First, he said he had judged the other person's expertise on the topic unfairly, and he felt guilty for having bad thoughts about his friend during the argument. Next, he said he felt ridiculous because the argument had no impact whatsoever on his life. No one was even asking his opinion and it had nothing to do with him.

Today, we can chuckle about that day, because he learned a valuable lesson and shared that lesson with me, and I learned from his lesson how to "stay in my own lane". My friend said one of the valuable things he also learned was to forgive himself and just make better decisions in the future. Worrying about other people's opinions does us a disservice! I know now, what someone else thinks of me is none of my business. Knowing that released me emotionally from caring about other people's opinions about me.

Music and Trauma

Music as a therapeutic agent has been used to support trauma recovery on an individual and societal level. After the terrorist attacks on 9/11, after Hurricane Katrina in New Orleans, and for soldiers with traumatic injury (Weidlein, 2021). Music really does help me! I played football for 22 years so a lot of my memory is shot due to concussions. So, I started writing music as a way to help me remember traumatic situations and how I overcame them! According to the American Music Therapy Association (2021), music is therapeutic for sexual trauma survivors in the following ways:

- An outlet for non-verbal expressions of emotions associated with sexual violence
- Reduces stress and anxiety
- Lifts mood and positively affects emotions
- Creates active participation in therapy and recovery
- Increased confidence and feelings of empowerment and control.
- Better overall health and wellness, such as lowered heart rate and blood pressure and works as a muscle relaxer.

Improvisation and songwriting are two essential ways music therapy addresses trauma. Writing music for me is a way to journal my feelings in a way that lets me know I am okay, I remember what happened, and I am okay today. Music also helps emotional and physical intimacy for couples, as it provides meaningful together time in a creative and positive way. I love to share music with my family and friends because it is time set aside for relaxation.

Writing music enables me to put words together in a way that was difficult for me to do otherwise. Music therapy gets through to a trauma survivor, sometimes better than any other treatment strategy. A review of the literature using keywords trauma and music identified studies that found that survivors of childhood sexual trauma listened to music more often than individuals without childhood sexual trauma (Greenberg et al., 2016; Horden, 2000).

Balance of Happiness

There are so many things in life over which we have no control. Fortunately, for me, I get to help others as a profession. Balance starts with mindfulness. Take a second and consider something you do on a daily basis that no one has to ask you to do or tell you

o. Then simply ask yourself if you do it with love and good intenon. For me, I like to garden, spiritually bathe, take a walk, and
ave a wonderful cup of coffee. Those three activities ground me
nd provide me with comfort, peace, and quiet. Before recovery, I
idn't even know what self-love or self-care meant.

 you'll notice, all three of those activities are free; well, a small
rice for a cup of coffee with my favorite cinnamon-hazelnut
reamer. The idea behind the concept of happiness and balance is
hat BALANCE is a priority. When we have balance, we have more
appiness in our lives. Think about these aspects of your life:
amily, Social, Career, Exercise, Hobbies, Spirituality, and Health.

ow, start a self-dialog and write down a list of categories under
ach one of those aspects just mentioned. If you find one has an
mpty category, you know that is your starting point. Then ask
ourself if it is something you enjoy, love, or makes you happy. If
at category is only so/so to you, think about it and put something
se in its place that makes you happy. Ask yourself if you would do
 without being asked. Simply prioritize your categories and make
re they are filled with love and acceptance.

nagine a life full of things you love, enjoy, and that bring you
appiness. What if you found a way to eat healthily and therefore
rticipate in loving your body? What if you found a way to exerse that you actually love? What if you socialized with people you
ust and who genuinely care about you? What if putting on an old
ir of ripped-up jeans feels good? You may even have to consider
 change of career if the one you have is making you unhappy. I
ow that is no easy feat, but what is the point of living each day if
 is filled with something that you don't want to do? Balance brings
ppiness.

fe is basically a balancing act. If you have children, you have to
lance family and your job; if your parents are elderly, you
lance leisure time and family; if you are recovering from sexual
uma, you have to balance your life with your recovery

program. For me, happiness is balancing my condition as a survivor with my positive coping resources, such as therapy, meetings, and self-love. If your positive support system outweighs the negatives in your life, you will be coping with sexual trauma effectively. The important thing to remember here is that it is a combination of things; never one thing, it is a balancing act between the two. Effectively coping with trauma can bring happiness, and pride, it is balance.

How to Thrive

If you were a tree, would you be growing tall, branching out, and resilient in a flood or a drought? Or would all of your leaves fall off and you wither away when the rains came? This is the difference between surviving and thriving. We know people are much more complicated than trees, but the truth is that two people under similar circumstances can react differently. You have to choose to thrive. It is an outlook and attitude about life, and in order to thrive in this fast-paced society, you have to take action and stay connected to your body. Training your body, mind, and spirit to thrive on a daily basis doesn't have to be complicated.

Here is One Month of Daily of Activities to Turn Surviving into Thriving

- Center yourself when you first wake up and put forth your intentions for the day. Spend a few moments in prayer or meditation and connect to your inner sanctuary while imagining how you want your day to play out.
- Let go of any expectations placed on you by your family, friends, coworkers, society, and yourself. Only set expectations that are in alignment with positive energy.
- Listen with intent and without judging. It is almost natural for our minds to judge and analyze. Deep breath and let

your mind fully listen and let go of any inclinations to pounce into judgment.

- Spend some time with nature, as previously mentioned. The birds, the beach, the trees, the water, all are teachers, and being with them brings enlightenment and gratitude.
- Nourish your body with whole foods. Thriving on what the Earth supplies instead of processed food from factories is what God and the Universe intended for us to do.
- When life seems too serious, get up and do a jig. That's what the saying "shake it off" means. When anxiety is weighing you down, put on your favorite music and dance.
- Unplug or disconnect. Bask in the stillness and relish your inner peace. Turn off your cell phone and step away from the laptop. Tune into God, Mother Earth, or the Universe and the Love within you.
- Stop whining. Focus more on the good things in life and less on what happened to you and how troubled the world is. There is enough of that to go around for everyone just watching one hour of the evening news. Don't be surprised when you find out that positive attracts positive and abundance to your life.
- Social media Detox and TV too. It is akin to dissociation burying yourself or binging on episodes. Advertisements and fear-based stories are not the best medicine for the soul.
- Say thank you to those you love and for the people that show you support. Appreciation is food for the soul.
- Try a new activity. The universe has so much to offer, so don't stop exploring the endless possibilities for expanding your spirit.
- Read a book, oh, I see you are reading a book; wonderful!
- Make family time, happy time. Focus on the quality of the time with family, not the quantity.
- An attitude of gratitude! Even in our darkest hours, we can find something to be grateful for.

- Journal five minutes per day and write a gratitude list each night of three things. Bear witness to your growth.
- Make a daily action plan by setting achievable goals. Break them down into bite-size pieces and watch them all add up.
- Design your own mantra. "I am strong" "I love" "I am a survivor". Write mantras for areas you may need a boost in from time to time. Repeat these affirmations regularly.
- Learn how to do something new. Have you ever baked a cake from scratch? DIY projects enhance self-esteem and self-worth.
- Put the shoe on the other foot. Take the time to imagine what someone else is going through and your empathy will increase.
- Compliment your family. Show them your light and how it shines.
- Plant herbs or anything that grows. Watching something transform is all-inspiring.
- Take "me-time". Spend time each day getting to know yourself better, soon you will find you always have a trustworthy friend around.
- Sleep in once a week even if it is not on your to-do list; put it on there.
- You know what they say about assuming. They are based on ego, not reality or truth.
- Rearrange your to-do list by doing the things you least want to do first. The day plays out easier.
- Replace fear with faith. Be mindful in every moment and ask yourself "why fear?" when you have faith.
- Stick with the winners. Look for the good in each situation, no matter how difficult. Pessimism shortens your life.
- "Laugh and the whole world laughs with you" is so true. Laughter is the body's built-in antidepressant.

- Discover your purpose. Not necessarily in life, all at once, but for the day. Seek out things you feel passionate about.
- Never forget the power of random acts of kindness and paying it forward.
- Love sex and love yourself!

Be You Be Happy

ccepting life's realities sounds like it shouldn't be that difficult. owever, many people tend to have their own take on reality. It ay be rooted in resentment, denial, regret, disappointment, ame, or they are living in tomorrow: waiting for the kids to leave ome, waiting to retire, you know the drill. Failing the reality check the reason that the suit in the closet hasn't fit in 15 years, but you ll yourself it is motivation to get back into it. There are better ans for your life than living some fictional version of yourself in ur own head. Even though survivors of sexual trauma have had rrible situations, the first step in recovery is acknowledging it for actly what it was.

ere are ten ways to cope with reality, even the parts you hate, and u go about changing your reality to one that you really want:

1. Self-acceptance. Self-acceptance is valuing unconditionally all parts of your life and who you are. That means accepting all of yourself, including your body, your trauma, and the good things about you. It also means accepting the parts of you that need improvement. Acceptance is a state of mind.
2. Accept and recognize your reality. Sometimes, this is the hardest thing to do when you have a past full of pain. But, recognizing your current reality can lead to loving yourself and a brighter future. Working with, understanding, and accepting reality gives your purpose and is practical as

well. It will help you to be wise about your dreams and then how to achieve them.

3. Radical honesty on a daily basis. When you can admit to your attempt to make things seem not as they are, you can then create a better tomorrow. Refusing to believe your present reality, especially if it is an unhappy one, will not make it disappear. You have to go through the bad stuff and it will open up the road to the good stuff.

4. Identify the part you play in life. To accept what your reality truly is, you have to recognize the role you play in it; good, bad, or otherwise, it's your reality. Now you can ask yourself how to foster success because you know what's in your hands.

5. Admit when you're wrong. Things can't get right if you will not admit when you're wrong. Mistakes are pathways to growth. They are opportunities to learn. Only you truly know your reality, so you are the only one that can change it. Set your priorities and go for it!

6. Own your successes. You need to own all parts of your reality and that means patting yourself on the back for a job well done! It is good to own all of your outcomes, including the ones that don't work out so well, sometimes these are the most important things to learn because they will teach you how to do better the next time.

7. Don't let anyone stand in your way, but accepting feedback is a sign of emotional maturity.

8. Count your blessings. In order to face your reality, remember you are a survivor turned thriver! Jot down your strengths, values, and achievements. This will improve your self-confidence and self-worth. Spend far less time counting your insecurities.

9. Adopt a non-bias attitude. Don't get stuck in a life you think you are supposed to live, but in the one, you are meant to live. Judgments make you reality-blind. You can pretend all you want that you have no biases, but the truth

is we all do. Once you recognize and understand them, you can let them go.

10. Accept that what happened to you will always be part of your reality. Embrace it or just know that struggling is part of everyone's lives, learning how to confront them and heal is to truly live. If what happened to me didn't happen to me, I may not be in the position to help others like me, by writing this book.

Living Stress-Free of Sexual Depression

Imagine this: You and your intimate partner are in bed together and things are heating up. You are kissing and touching each other, your clothes are coming off, and suddenly, your past flashes back. You can almost hear your abuser, and you feel like running away. The next thing you know is that you are stressed to the max! You feel it in your body. You feel it in your soul. You start to wonder if you are going to be able to keep going. Suddenly, the last thing on your mind is sex, even though you are right in the middle of it. Whether your stress is from a traumatic experience or you have a huge work project you have to get done, it spills over into other parts of your life, like the bedroom. It can make you anxious, irritable, and upset, and it's famous for killing your sex drive.

Sex is important to any intimate relationship, and if it's leading to less sex with your lover, because of the amount of stress you have, it will definitely put your relationship to the test. Some people effectively manage stress and have learned how to compartmentalize their emotions, like leaving your work at the job. But many with a history of sexual trauma, when you want to be sexual, it triggers your stress hormones and consumes your mind. It can be hard to stay in the mood and not want to put having sex on the back corner.

If you find yourself having difficulty in the bedroom, because you get stuck between your two ears, or you are hesitant altogether, you can learn to intentionally destress yourself before sex. Before you transition into foreplay or getting in the mood, take a moment to decompress. Essential oil and a tub bath work for me. Manly men can take lavender-scented baths, too! Music can set the mood and help relax you as well.

Practicing self-care will boost your self-worth and make a tremendous difference in the way you will feel for the rest of your evening. On top of that, you can do something relaxing and sensual with your lover like massage or sweet talk, and mutual breathing exercises. Include your partner in the decompression exercise and most of all talk to each other about any anxiety. You can also get into the habit of touching each other passionately, and not having it lead somewhere every time. It is a great way to ramp up your sex life and build some healthy sexual tension.

Take note if you are stressed out because you feel your partner pressuring you to have sex and you don't want to disappoint them. Communication is the most important element of healthy sex. While you are having sex, focus on the sensations happening in the present moment. Mindfulness in the bedroom is a great way to allay those intrusive memories and keep them from standing in the way of your romantic time together.

Don't Stop Kissing

There is such a market out there as to how you can have a better orgasm, a better relationship, and better sex. But we don't often get the details on how we can have a better understanding of our most embarrassing questions and our deepest desires. It seems as though most of us have been in relationships where we have personally witnessed the slowdown of kissing (it is the cousin to sexual slowdown). Even though it seems fairly common for those juicy lips to stop calling, it doesn't mean you are doomed to a relationship without kissing. Kissing seems to slow down from when a couple first starts dating. First kisses are magical; the excitement, attraction on, potential, and the chemistry. In the beginning, it seems as though you kiss for hours. But, with time the novelty of kissing wears off, we get used to the whole process and it becomes less thrilling. Like anything we experience on a regular basis, that's just the way life is. Plus, how realistic is it to spend that much time kissing every day? Although it is fun, it is not really sustainable. It doesn't mean you are not as in love or that you're bored, all it means is fanning the sexual flames requires a little more effort by both people.

Traumatic stress can distract you from being present during sex. I call it robotic sex. Being fully present and diving into the pleasure is what feels good. If the sex is going to be mechanical, you might as well use a vibrator or your hand. I have talked to a lot of people that told me they stopped kissing during sex a long time ago. What? Kissing is sensual, exciting, and passionate. Frankly, it's a turn on! There is a purpose for kissing. Now I am referring to French kissing because there are other types of kissing such as those you give your kids or your friends.

One of the biggest turn-ons when it comes to the first make-out session is the buildup, the uncertainty, and the anticipation about when and how it is going to happen. Just wondering how the person is going to kiss is a juicy thought. The good news is that feeling can be recaptured by surprising your lover with a bit of tongue. Maybe you see that person just sitting on the couch reading a book and feel a bit of a sexiness surge; perfect timing for an unexpected slew of kisses. How about talking about it? I don't mean the serious "let's have a discussion" I mean, "Hey you, I'm seriously in the mood for some heavy kissing right now!" The element of surprise is a turn on.

Why do so many couples stop kissing with their tongues?

- Is it time-consuming? Sometimes, couples have kids in the

picture, and bam, there goes their time. It is important to make time for kissing.

- Do you find it unnecessary? Usually, when you first hook up with someone, both people get to first base (the French kiss). That is how they show they are attracted to each other. I mean in the beginning, a bad kisser can be a real deal-breaker. But, continuing to kiss each other or the person you are having sex with can really get your motor running. Once two people are together for any length of time, they are commonly comfortable enough to say "Do you want to do it" and the kissing part has gone right out of the window.

- Is it because you look at it as expending unnecessary energy? I say it's energy well spent. To serve its purpose, it should be authentic. At the very least couples should talk about their feelings when it comes to kissing. Even if you're with someone for years, make-out sessions are still important!

- With time together, do you feel that you show your affections better in other ways, like cooking a nice meal together, and taking a walk together? I say poppycock! Kiss in the kitchen while you're cooking, and stop on that beach walk for a kiss. It keeps you intimately participating in the relationship and less of the friend-zone behaving couple.

The Importance of Touch

Expressing your intimacy sexually is a part of every healthy rel^{...}tionship. But what if because of your past you are not a touc^{...} person or having sex is emotionally challenging for you? Learn^{...} express yourself sexually through intimate touching is possib^{...} even or especially if it is not about having sex. We are sexual bein^{...} who have sex, not because of sex. Sex is not the be-all of relatio^{...} ships, yes, it is important, but it is not the only way to physica^{...}

xpress yourself to someone with whom you are involved. Who oesn't have a smile creep across their face when they see a couple alking down the street holding hands? Holding hands can also be a private, even if you are just sitting together watching Netflix. It is asy enough and believe it or not, it stimulates the immediate elease of mood-enhancing endorphins. Parents hold their children's hands, not only for protection but to show affection.

ow about cuddling? I think trouble is amidst a relationship when uddling goes out the window. Wrapping your arms and legs round your person not only connects you physically but spiritually, sychologically, and emotionally. Take turns on who plays the rger spoon for fun. Touching skin-to-skin is part of the human ondition, it is meant to be. Touching a bare leg, or running your umb across your lover's lips, feeling their hair, is an expression of traction, love, passion, and lets them know you are there with em and for them. Did you know that cuddling actually boosts the mune system (Sheppard, 2020)?

ne of the best things about touching is that you can express yourlf without words, without having to go out to dinner or buy gifts. uch transmits a strong sense of acceptance and care. There are any positive emotions associated with touch, such as contentent, relaxation, and peppiness. Give the gift of touch! Touching akes you feel connected and is a simple way to let go of the day's ess.

en when it's not about sex, non-intimate touch speaks a thound words. Here are some great ways to express emotional intiacy through touch:

- Back rubs: Massaging your partner's head, back, the whole body shows them you support them and you love them. If someone you care about has had a bad day, offer a shoulder rub, it lets them know you care enough to want to help them feel better. I have a friend that every time she gets a foot rub, it leads to other things. She doesn't know why, and it is never planned, it just happens for her. Just make sure you talk about it first. Especially for victims of trauma, massage needs to be thoroughly planned out.

- Sitting close enough to touch: It is like holding hands or hugging. Leaning against someone is incredibly affectionate and a great way to connect. Playing footsie under the dinner table, anyone?
- Tickling, if you like it, and make sure the person you are tickling likes it. Again, communication is everything.
- Give hugs when someone comes home.
- Touch a person on the arm when making a point or if in a low-level argument (not a big argument).
- Bury your head into your partner's shoulder and hold still for a few moments.
- With consent and discussion, many couples enjoy light spankings.

Coming Out of Your Sexual Shell

There are many useful ways to increase your and your partner sexual comfort. One of them is to talk during sex. I don't mea "dirty talk" (that can be fun too), I mean a direct conversation th is meant to quiet your partner's inner anxiety, and it will help wi yours too. For instance, you can tell them if you don't mind certa things "It's okay with me if you touch yourself, I like it". After all, is a way of giving them permission to enjoy what's happening much as you do. Just make sure that you are both comfortable wi your version of sex talk.

After communication is established, finding the right phrases an words will come easily. Most of the time, sexual inhibitions ste from basic insecurities or a lack of confidence. If you make t person, you're with feel like the Sex God or Goddess, they will fe like one too. Making someone feel sexy while you are making lov all the better for it. Take it slowly, and learn how to talk about the ways you want to be touched or penetrated. This way you both can choose what feels best to each other and introduce new ways of touching as the relationship progresses. You can experiment with different degrees of pressure, speed, and slowly build your sexual repertoire.

Another big-time anxiety arousing emotion is body image disturbance. People uncomfortable with their bodies; maybe they have a few extra pounds, or not enough pounds, and they absolutely will not have sex with the lights on. If this is the case, maybe they won't mind a candle to start out with. Just spend time complimenting them, and letting them know that you don't mind the pounds, wrinkles, or any of their beautiful imperfections. We all have them! Plus, sometimes with light dirty talk, the person stops focusing on their body anxiety and feels less nervous about adding some light.

Another thing you can do to help your partner come out of their sexual shell is to do to them what they are doing to you. Oftentimes, during sex, someone will touch you where and how they like to be touched. It creates a safe atmosphere because they are in a sense teaching you what they like. Without saying anything, they will have had complete control over the foreplay and may want to spend more time in it.

Brainstorming fantasies together is a great way to shed your sexual shell. Talk about what type of movies you like and don't like, and then figure out how to make the fantasy a reality. The two of you can list your fantasies and give them to each other to read in private, alone. Then a day or two later who knows what will happen. The most important aspect of breaking your sexual shell or your partner's is by increasing the feeling of being sexually safe. Low sex esteem is caused by anxiety, so getting turned on can only happen when both people feel completely safe, then all inhibitions can be dropped.

Everyone has their own unique connection to their sexuality, which is what makes it such a beautiful and special journey. No matter how difficult your experience and barriers, coming out of your sexual shell can be both gratifying and liberating. Here are some ways to break out of your sexual shell and find the happiness you deserve:

- Make your own decisions, if you want to have more satisfaction or enhanced arousal, it is up to you, no one else! While you share your sexuality with other people in your lifetime, by nature it is empowering because as a survivor you are in control of what you do to and with your body. If you decide to explore your sexual cravings on a deeper level, it all starts with you. When you come up with ideas about what you are in the mood for, you will have pleasurable results.
- Explore your own sexual anatomy. Absolutely a must. Get yourself a mirror and take a look down there. Forget the stigma and shame and love your body and appreciate it. Get to know where everything is and what you're working with before you invite someone else to do it. It is called being healthy.
- Become one with your body. We are just moving so fast these days, always connected to something smart (phones, TVs, iPads, etc.) that will hardly leave any time for ourselves. Slow your roll and become connected on a deeper level with your own body. Sleep naked, or go barefoot, dance, and lay down in the grass, feel it. If trauma made you lose your connection to your body, these easy activities will rekindle that relationship or start one you may never have known.
- Show your body you love it. Embrace any of your gorgeous imperfections. It is not easy when our Facebook feeds are inundated with unrealistic images that pull on our inner emotions. Your body is a beautiful thing, look at

it in a full-length mirror, and speak kind and positive affirmations to it, treat your body the way it deserves to be treated. Finding out you are beautiful doesn't have to come from someone else. It comes from within.

- Let go of shyness. It is fine to keep private moments, but using a vibrator, looking at sexy books, or whatever gets you in the mood, is no longer taboo. Have fun experimenting on your own; it may help your relationship with your body and therefore, help the rest of you.

Final Thoughts

Who am I

Who am I (I am who I am)
I am love
I am pain
I am honest
I am awake

I am T.R.U.T.H. (Talk real understand truth
hurts)
I am reality
I am love
I am faith

No one can control me cause I am my future
I am who I am, I AM ME! No one else
That's who I am

A poem by
Lavender Jones M.D.

motional reactions of sexual trauma victims vary from person to
rson, but there is no doubt that the violence is life-changing. If
u are a survivor, I hope the information provided in this book
lps you to know that your reactions are not crazy; they are the

reactions of a person traumatized and they are normal. Thi wasn't and never will have been any fault of yours. You were over powered in many ways by the vicious and demonic acts c someone else.

Regardless of gender, race, age, or religion, rape can happen t anyone. One out of every three women and one out of every si men at some time in their life are assaulted sexually. It is hard t fathom how someone can commit such acts, and often to thos most vulnerable, our children. It is a far cry from being fair, and am sure you felt like life dealt you a dirty hand, but YOU ARE . SURVIVOR! You are courageous and strong.

Survivors/victims of sexual abuse can have a multitude c concerns, sexually. Some individuals may avoid sexual contact, an others may use sex as a coping mechanism. It is important t realize that sexual abuse and sex are not the same thing. Som sexual activities can trigger flashbacks and make it hard t engage in.

Sexual healing is not an overnight process, but it is possible. Yc can live a perfectly healthy, happy, joyous, and free sexual life th fills you with satisfaction and peace. Communication can't be ove stated, and make sure not to rush yourself, move at your pace; yc are in control over your body, no one else is. You have the right say "no" anytime before or during, and "no" does mean "no".

Enjoying a happy sex life is a huge part of life satisfaction. No o should have to go through life without experiencing the wonders a climax, sensual touching, masturbation, and all of the oth wonderful things you can think of that feels good to you. Wheth you have been with the same person for two weeks or twenty yea you may have some issues surrounding your sex life as a couple.

Having a healthy sex life has been associated with better over health and wellness, including a boost to your immune system, a heart health. There are those who think a happy sex life is based

ow often they have sex, and some think mutual orgasms or
multiple orgasms make for a happy sex life. Like everything else in
life, it is the quality, not the quantity of sex you have to be happy in
sex. What matters is that each person having sex feels comfortable
and safe and the only way that happens is by communicating. By
the way, it may seem easier sometimes to fake like you are enjoying
yourself, and women can even fake an orgasm. It is much better to
talk about why it isn't working for you than to pretend it is. By
trying to avoid hurting someone's feelings, you are selling yourself
and them short. Maybe you are tired and just want to get it over
with....then don't do it.

We already went over not skimping on the foreplay, but don't skip
on the after play either. The time spent after sex is just as important. It is an important time to keep touching each other in an
emotionally intimate way. Physically touching some parts of the
body after sex can be very ticklish, as those areas are full of blood
and very sensitive. If you just roll over and fall right asleep, you are
missing out on the chance to get closer and to know each other
better and validate your feelings for one another.

If you are planning on a pleasure-filled evening, build up each
other's desire and anticipation throughout the day. Give a quick
phone call, leave a card on the breakfast table, just give each other
that look as if you can't wait to be together. Build up your night in
your own mind too, arousal will heighten if you let your thoughts
wander about the forthcoming activities.

There is no quick fix or instruction book for healing, but there is
recovery and it is lifelong. No one can teach you to heal, so it can
be a frightening situation. There are not five easy steps to take or a
pill. But healing is happening and talking about it is the most
important thing you can do in recovery. It will eventually become a
the experience, an awful one, but nonetheless, the past.

The best knowledge anyone can gain or have comes from your
experience in life, and it is that experience that makes up your

character and gives you a deeper understanding of personal pain than others who have not suffered in the way that you have. What happened to you or someone you know was traumatic, and often we don't know the extent of its effects immediately. But, pretending it never happened or ignoring it doesn't make it go away, the feelings get worse with time, and it can turn into a full-fledged mental illness.

It is hard to believe such memories are real, but the memories can hurt as much as when they happened. Traumatic memories retraumatize the victim and without help can be paralyzing. Sometimes the images can be blocked from our minds, but they resurface in other areas of our lives. I felt so trapped in them, that I felt like Tom Hanks in the movie Castaway! But guess what? You're NOT crazy; you dealt with crazy!

After sexual trauma, survivors can feel numb and stuck thinking about what they could have done differently to change the outcome. It can be hard to focus, do well at school or work, and the worst part is the constant reminders while you are busy trying to reclaim a normal life. Nightmares, eating or swallowing problems, anxiety and depression are all common symptoms of sexual abuse. Now is the time to be gentle with yourself. It is important to go through the grieving process. Many have to grieve the loss of childhood and for many the only family they ever knew was chaotic and violent, full of secrets, or a house of horrors.

The worst thing you can do to yourself is fear asking for help. Maybe you didn't realize the trauma was the foundation for most of your insecurities, fears, and social problems. Maybe you found solace in alcohol or drugs, or maybe you have ended up in a lifestyle you wouldn't wish on your worst enemy, or maybe you became such an overachiever, but can never seem to feel like you are enough. Whatever your condition is, I pray you find your answers and if even a few were provided by reading this book, then my life has been enriched and purposeful. Thank you, for surviving.

For friends, colleagues, and relatives of someone who has been assaulted, sexually:

- Don't blame or judge them. It is never their fault.
- Listen without asking for details and please don't ask them why they didn't stop it.
- Offer support, practical in nature, such as taking them to appointments or sleeping on their couch. Making a home-cooked meal and going grocery shopping are also supportive measures.
- Respect whether or not they decide to call the police.
- Be Careful, they may not want to be touched physically. You may be inclined to want to give them a hug or hold them in some way, also if it is someone you are intimate with do not pressure them to get back to having sex.
- Don't tell them they will get over it, or to forget about it. Listen and be patient. Find the nearest sexual assault and rape resources, call them yourself, and get informed.

You never have to be alone. There are organizations available or you can call the **National Sexual Assault Hotline**. Free. Confidential. 24/7 at 1-800-656-4673 or click on the following link: https://www.rainn.org/ if you or anyone you know needs help. Support is available right now from the **National Domestic Violence Hotline**. Call 1-800-799-7233 or chat online.

Sources

---

merican Association of University Women. (2011). *Crossing the ne: Sexual Harassment at School*. Published.

merican Music Therapy Association. (2021). *Music therapy.* tps://www.musictherapy.org/

abbel, S. (2013). Trauma: Childhood sexual abuse. *Psychology day.* https://www.psychologytoday.com/us/blog/somatic-ychology/201303/trauma-childhood-sexual-abuse

rody, S. (2010). *The relative health benefits of different sexual activities.* n.jsexmed.org/article/S1743-6095(15)32977-5/fulltext

hild Welfare Information Gateway. (2018). *Trauma-focused cognitive havioral therapy: A primer for child welfare professionals*. Washington, C: U.S. Department of Health and Human Services, Children's ıreau/

ancy, S. (2009). *The Trauma Myth*. New York: Basic Books.

ohen, J. A., Mannarino, A. P., & Iyengar, S. (2011). Community atment of posttraumatic stress disorder for children exposed to imate partner violence. *Archives of Pediatrics & Adolescent Medicine,* 5(1), 16–21. DOI: 10.1001/archpediatrics.2010.247

Cohen, J. A., & Mannarino, A. P. (2015). Trauma-focused cognitive behavioral therapy for traumatized children and families. *Child and Adolescent Psychiatric Clinic of North America, 24*(3), 557–570. doi 10.1016/j.chc.2015.02.005.

Department of Justice, Office of Justice Programs, Bureau of Justice Statistics, (2019). *Sexual Assault of Young Children as Reported to Law Enforcement.*

Durshlag, R., & Goswami, S. (2008). *Deconstructing the demand for prostitution: Preliminary insight from interviews with Chicago men who purchase sex.* http://g.virbcdn.com/_f/files/40/FileItem-149406 DeconstructingtheDemandForProstitution.pdf

Farley, M. (2003). *Prostitution, trafficking, and traumatic stress.* New York, NY: Routledge

Foster, J. & Hagedorn, W. (2014). Through the eyes of the wounded: a narrative analysis of children's sexual abuse experiences and recovery process. *Journal of Child Sexual Abuse 23*(5) 538–557. Doi: 10.1080/10538712.2014.918072

Greenberg, D. M., Jurist, E., Rosenberg, N., Müllensiefen, D, Lamb, M., & Rentfrow, P. (2016). *Linking childhood trauma to music engagement in adulthood: Implications for clinical practice.* Poster presented at the 2016 meeting of the Psychodynamic Psychoanalytic Research Society, New York. Google Scholar

Herman J. (2003). Introduction: hidden in plain sight: clinical observations on prostitution. In: *Prostitution, Trafficking and Trauma Stress,* Farley M, ed. Binghamton, N.Y.: Haworth Press, pp 1-13.

Holly, K. (2012). Effects of verbal abuse on children, women and men. *HealthyPlace.* https://www.healthyplace.com/abuse/verbal abuse/effects-of-verbal-abuse-on-children-women-and-men

Horden, P. (2000). Music as medicine. *Ashgate.* https://book google.com/books

Huh, H., Kim, S., Yu, J., & Chae, J. (2014). Childhood trauma and adult interpersonal relationship problems in patients with depression and anxiety disorders. *Ann Gen Psychiatry (13)*:26. doi:10.1186/s12991-014-0026-y

Carlos, S. (2019). A lesson on why victims of sexual assault stay silent. *Daily Aztec*. https://thedailyaztec.com/94723/el-alma/opinion-a-lesson-on-why-victims-of-sexual-assault-stay-silent/

King, B. (2009). *Human sexuality today* (6th ed.). Upper Saddle River, NJ: Pearson.

Kristense, E. & Lau, M. (2011) Sexual function in women with a history of intrafamilial childhood sexual abuse. *Sexual and Relationship Therapy 26*(3) 229-241. DOI: 10.1080/14681994.2011.622264

Krueger R. (2016). *Diagnosis of hypersexual or compulsive sexual behavior can be made using ICD-10 and DSM-5 despite rejection of this diagnosis by the American Psychiatric Association.* onlinelibrary.wiley.com/doi/epdf/10.1111/add.13366

Letourneau, E. & O'Donohue, W. (1993). Sexual Desire Disorders. In O'Donohue, W. and Geer, J. (Eds.) *Handbook of Sexual Dysfunctions*, Boston: Allyn and Bacon.

Long, L. L., Burnett, J. A., & Thomas, R. V. (2006). *Sexuality counseling: An integrative approach.* Upper Saddle River, NJ: Pearson

Maltz, W. (2002). Treating the sexual intimacy concerns of sexual abuse survivors. *Sexual and Relationship Therapy, 17*(4), 321-327.

Rape, Abuse and Incest National Network. (2016). *Statistics.* https://www.rainn.org/statistics

Renewal Lodge.com (2019). *Five ways quitting drinking affects your brain.* https://www.renewallodge.com/5-ways-quitting-drinking-affects-your-brain/

Gilbert, C. (2020). *Forest bathing for trauma recovery.* https://cyndigilbert.ca/forest-bathing-for-trauma-recovery/

Grof, S. & Grof, C. (2021). *Principles of Holotropic Breathwork* http://www.holotropic.com/wp-content/uploads/2017/12/Principles-of-Holotropic-Breathwork.pdf

Sheppard, S. (2020). What Is the physical touch love language *VerywellMind.com* https://www.verywellmind.com/physical-touch-love-language-4797513

Stark, C. & Hodgson, C (2003). Sister oppressions: a comparison of wife battering and prostitution. In: *Prostitution, Trafficking, and Traumatic Stress*, Farley M, ed. Binghamton, N.Y.: Haworth Press pp17-32.

Su Y, S., Veeravagu, A., & Grant G. (2016). Neuroplasticity after traumatic brain injury. In: Laskowitz D, Grant G, editors. *Translational Research in Traumatic Brain Injury*. Boca Raton (FL): CRC Press/Taylor and Francis Group. Chapter 8. PMID: 26583189.

United States Department of Health and Human Services, Administration for Children and Families, Administration on Children, Youth and Families, Children's Bureau. (2018). *Child Maltreatment Survey*, 2016. https://www.acf.hhs.gov/cb/data-research/child-maltreatment

Weidlein,(2021). Music therapy addresses trauma. *MajoringinMusic.com*. https://majoringinmusic.com/music-therapy-addresses-trauma/

Wentland J. & Reissing E. (2014). Casual sexual relationships: Identifying definitions for one-night stands, booty calls, f--- buddies, and friends with benefits. *Can J Hum Sex.* *23*(3):167-17 doi:10.3138/cjhs.2744

Made in the USA
Columbia, SC
02 September 2024